American Birding Association

Field Guide

to Birds of

the Carolinas

Nate Swick

PHOTOGRAPHS BY
Brian E. Small
AND OTHERS

Scott & Nix, Inc.
NEW YORK

PUBLISHED BY SCOTT & NIX, INC.
150 W 28TH ST, STE 1900
NEW YORK, NY 10001
SCOTTANDNIX.COM

FIRST EDITION 2016
THIRD PRINTING 2020

ISBN 978-1-935622-63-5

AMERICAN BIRDING ASSOCIATION, INC.
800-850-2473
ABA.ORG

SCOTT & NIX, INC. BOOKS
ARE DISTRIBUTED TO THE TRADE BY

INDEPENDENT PUBLISHERS GROUP (IPG)
814 NORTH FRANKLIN STREET
CHICAGO, IL 60610
800-888-4741
IPGBOOK.COM

PRINTED IN CHINA

Contents

The American Birding Association inspires all people to enjoy and protect wild birds.

The ABA represents the North American birding community and supports birders through publications, conferences, workshops, events, partnerships, and networks.

The ABA's education programs promote birding skills, ornithological knowledge, and the development of and implementation of a conservation ethic.

The ABA encourages birders to apply their skills to help conserve birds and their habitats, and we represent the interests of birders in planning and legislative arenas.

We welcome all birders as members.

THE AMERICAN BIRDING ASSOCIATION CODE OF ETHICS

Everyone who enjoys birds and birding must always respect wildlife, its environment, and the rights of others. In any conflict of interest between birds and birders, the welfare of the birds and their environment comes first.

CODE OF BIRDING ETHICS

1. Promote the welfare of birds and their environment.

   1(a) Support the protection of important bird habitat.

   1(b) To avoid stressing birds or exposing them to danger, exercise restraint and caution during observation, photography, sound recording, or filming.

Limit the use of recordings and other methods of attracting birds, and never use such methods in heavily birded areas, or for attracting any species that is Threatened, Endangered,

or of Special Concern, or is rare in your local area; Keep
well back from nests and nesting colonies, roosts, display areas,
and important feeding sites. In such sensitive areas, if there
is a need for extended observation, photography, filming,
or recording, try to use a blind or hide, and take advantage of
natural cover.

Use artificial light sparingly for filming or photography,
especially for close-ups.

> 1(c) Before advertising the presence of a rare bird, evaluate
> the potential for disturbance to the bird, its surroundings,
> and other people in the area, and proceed only if access
> can be controlled, disturbance minimized, and permission
> has been obtained from private land-owners. The sites
> of rare nesting birds should be divulged only to the proper
> conservation authorities.

> 1(d) Stay on roads, trails, and paths where they exist;
> otherwise keep habitat disturbance to a minimum.

2. Respect the law, and the rights of others.

> 2(a) Do not enter private property without the owner's
> explicit permission.

> 2(b) Follow all laws, rules, and regulations governing use of
> roads and public areas, both at home and abroad.

> 2(c) Practice common courtesy in contacts with other people.
> Your exemplary behavior will generate goodwill with birders
> and non-birders alike.

3. Ensure that feeders, nest structures, and other artificial bird
environments are safe.

> 3(a) Keep dispensers, water, and food clean, and free of decay
> or disease. It is important to feed birds continually during
> harsh weather.

> 3(b) Maintain and clean nest structures regularly.

> 3(c) If you are attracting birds to an area, ensure the birds
> are not exposed to predation from cats and other domestic
> animals, or dangers posed by artificial hazards.

4. Group birding, whether organized or impromptu, requires
special care.

Each individual in the group, in addition to the obligations spelled out in Items 1 and 2, has responsibilities as a Group Member.

4(a) Respect the interests, rights, and skills of fellow birders, as well as people participating in other legitimate outdoor activities. Freely share your knowledge and experience, except where code 1(c) applies. Be especially helpful to beginning birders.

4(b) If you witness unethical birding behavior, assess the situation, and intervene if you think it prudent. When interceding, inform the person(s) of the inappropriate action, and attempt, within reason, to have it stopped. If the behavior continues, document it, and notify appropriate individuals or organizations.

Group Leader Responsibilities [amateur and professional trips and tours].

4(c) Be an exemplary ethical role model for the group. Teach through word and example.

4(d) Keep groups to a size that limits impact on the environment, and does not interfere with others using the same area.

4(e) Ensure everyone in the group knows of and practices this code.

4(f) Learn and inform the group of any special circumstances applicable to the areas being visited (e.g. no tape recorders allowed).

4(g) Acknowledge that professional tour companies bear a special responsibility to place the welfare of birds and the benefits of public knowledge ahead of the company's commercial interests. Ideally, leaders should keep track of tour sightings, document unusual occurrences, and submit records to appropriate organizations.

Everyone who enjoys birds and birding must always respect wildlife, its environment, and the rights of others. The ABA Code of Ethics should be read, followed, and shared by all birders.

Please follow this code and distribute and teach it to others.

The American Birding Association's Code of Birding Ethics may be freely reproduced for distribution/dissemination. An electronic version may be found at aba.org/about/ethics.

Foreword

If you call either of the Carolinas home or just visit from time to time, you know that they have many charms. What you may not yet realize is just how good they are for birding. This book will open your eyes to a world of discoveries starting right at your doorstep. From the teeming marshes of the Low Country to the bonanza of breeding songbirds in the Great Smokies, there is a wealth of bird life to enjoy here all year long.

Like all the guides in this series, this book can help you do whatever you want with birding. Perhaps you enjoy birds a few days a year in your yard or local park and just want to know a little more about them and to know some of their names. Or maybe you want to dive deeper and really get familiar with the hundreds of amazing birds that call the Carolinas home for part or all of each year. Our aim is to meet you where you are and give you useful, reliable information and insight into birds and birding.

Author Nathan Swick, who manages social media for the American Birding Association and is both a dedicated birder and a skillful, patient teacher, is the perfect guide for those wanting to explore North or South Carolina birds. You're in very good hands with him. The gorgeous photography by Brian Small and others will not only aid your identifications—it will inspire you to get out and see more of these beautiful and fascinating creatures for yourself.

I invite you to visit the American Birding Association website (aba.org), where you'll find a wealth of free resources and ways to connect with the birding community that will also help you get the most from your birding in the Carolinas and beyond. Please consider becoming an ABA member yourself—one of the best parts of birding is joining a community of fun, passionate people.

Now get on out there! Enjoy this book. Enjoy the Carolinas. And most of all, enjoy birding!

Good birding,

Jeffrey A Gordon

Jeffrey A. Gordon, *President*
American Birding Association

Birds in the Carolinas

Taken together, North and South Carolina offer some of the most diverse habitats in eastern North America. From the high elevation spruce-fir forests of the Appalachians, to the windswept Outer Banks, to the cypress-lined swamps of the Savannah River Basin, to the sapphire waters of the Gulf Stream, birders in the Carolinas have no shortage of wonderful birding opportunities.

This richness, both of habitats and of species, has contributed to a long ornithological history in the Carolinas. From the 1700s, naturalists have spent time in these states, exploring, writing, and illustrating the birds here. Luminaries like John James Audubon, Alexander Wilson, and Mark Catesby have all spent time in the Carolinas, and William Brewster and Rev. John Bachman have made significant contributions to North America's ornithological history. *Carolinensis* is even part of the scientific name of common eastern species, such as White-breasted Nuthatch, Red-bellied Woodpecker, Gray Catbird, and others.

The scientific name of the dapper Gray Catbird, *Dumatella carolinensis*, refers to South Carolina, from whence came the first described specimen.

The Carolinas can be roughly divided into thirds. In the western third, the spine of the southern Appalachians, often referred to as the Blue Ridge Mountains, are the most significant geological feature and host the highest mountains east of the Mississippi River. Moving southeast, the mountains give way to the foothills of the Piedmont, where most of the region's human population is located. This is a region of broken forests, farms, fields, and development. Continuing east to the Coastal Plain, one can find more agricultural concerns, but also shrub ponds, longleaf pine forests, and wide, slow-moving rivers leading to the coast with its barrier islands and vast brackish marshes. With so much diversity throughout both states, it's no wonder that birding in the Carolinas is very good and often spectacular.

The cheery Northern Cardinal, North Carolina's state bird, is among the most familiar species throughout both states, and can be found in a wide variety of brushy habitats.

Birds in this Guide

As of 2016, 486 species have been recorded in the combined Carolinas—480 in North Carolina and 433 in South Carolina. The official list of both states consist of species that breed in the states, those that overwinter, those that pass through only in spring or fall, ocean-going birds only seen offshore, and a number of "vagrant" species, birds which occur in the Carolinas only on rare occasions and are not to be expected every year.

This guide contains accounts for 290 species that can be found in North and South Carolina. Most can be found in both states, but some are more common in one or the other. They are a selection of the most commonly encountered species, and contain a mix of breeding birds, wintering birds, and migrants. Nearly all of the species which routinely nest in either state are included. A dedicated birder willing to travel across the Carolinas could likely find all of them, and most certainly more, in one calendar year. For those interested, a full list of birds recorded in the Carolinas may be found on page 319.

South Carolina's state bird, the bold and curious Carolina Wren is hard to miss as it sings in woodlands throughout the Carolinas.

For the most part, birds are listed in this book in a slightly modified taxonomic order, as determined by the *Check-list of the American Ornithologist's Society*. While not always intuitive, this order reflects relationships between families of birds, and offers insight into their evolutionary history that are not obvious. Generally speaking, large birds come before smaller ones, and water birds before land birds. Taxonomic order can take some time to get used to, but I would urge anyone using this book to place it in a spot where you are inclined to take some time to page through it in your spare time. Doing so will help you to get comfortable not only with where groups of species can be found in the book before you need to identify a bird, but also you will begin to familiarize yourself with the individual birds, learning where and when to find them.

Each species account contains common and scientific names and average length and wingspan. Dimensions of each bird are less useful from an absolute perspective, but good for comparing expected sizes for two otherwise similar species.

Pectoral Sandpiper (this page) and Least Sandpiper (next page) are both streaky brown, with curved bills and yellow legs, but their size and shape are quite different, and obvious when the two species are seen together, as they often are.

For instance, Pectoral Sandpiper and Least Sandpiper share similar field marks but the former is significantly larger than the latter, which can be easily determined by comparing their respective lengths.

A short species account is included for every species, including distribution in the Carolinas, notable behavior, habitat preferences, time of year one is most likely to encounter them, and, when appropriate, vocalizations. For most species, suggestions for where in the Carolinas the species can be most reliably found is also included. For widespread species with broad preferences, only the habitat is required, but for those with more specific preferences, specific locations are noted. These can all be found on the map of North and South Carolina inside the front cover of this guide.

Each species account includes one or more photos of the species in plumages that one is likely to encounter in the Carolinas. Captions note field marks including plumage details and impression with the most important, or at least the most obvious, noted first. Terms like "large" and "small" are meant to be comparisons to similar species. Even a "small" duck like a Bufflehead is much larger in absolute size than a "large" finch, such as the Red Crossbill.

Bird Identification

When flipping through a field guide filled with hundreds of potential options for the mystery bird outside your window, it can be easy to feel overwhelmed. But it's important to remember that specific bird species often occupy specific spatial (location) and temporal (time of year) ranges. Not every bird included in this (or any) field guide is going to be present in your backyard in Winston-Salem on a brisk December morning, or on a beach near Charleston on a hot July day. Knowing where, when, and under what circumstances you can expect certain species allows you to narrow your options down quickly and easily. In a region like the Carolinas, with several distinct and broadly diverse ecotypes, this is especially useful, as some species never leave the mountains, while others are never found far from the shore.

Time of year is critical as well. While many birds are present in the Carolinas year-round, others are only present in the winter, breeding farther north. Still others decamp to the tropics in winter, visiting the region during the warm months when insect food is prevalent. And still others only pass through in spring and fall on their way to other places. Knowing when to expect certain species also helps to narrow down your possibilities and make identification simpler. It also keeps your birding exciting year-round, as a site in summer is likely to produce a completely different type of bird as the very same site in winter.

Be sure to take habitat into consideration. For the most part, birds are very reliable, particularly when it comes to the type of habitat they prefer. Many similar species will even segregate themselves into smaller patches of habitat within a larger mosaic. Take sparrows, for instance. Many novice birders find them to be difficult, but even similar species like Song Sparrow and Savannah Sparrow will typically be found in different places, the former preferring brushy hedges and the latter more open fields.

At the beach, Sanderlings will run among the crashing waves while Semipalmated Sandpipers will prefer sound-side sandbars, though the two may not be more than 100 yards apart. Paying attention to where you are finding certain birds in addition to what you are finding can be very rewarding, and will make you a more informed birder.

Once you've narrowed down your mystery bird to those most likely to occur in your area and local habitat, it's best to narrow it down further to family. Relative size and structure are good tools here, and be sure to pay attention to length of bill, tail, and legs. Also consider the bird's behavior, as size and structure is often directly connected to what the bird does and how it does it. Long-legged herons and egrets wade after fish on still water, sickle-winged swallows chase flying insects in open country, compact wrens scurry through dense vegetation. Having this information at your fingertips makes identifying birds much easier.

It's important to remember not to get too hung up on color when trying to identify a bird. While some species, like Painted Bunting, are a riot of color and hard to mistake for anything

The spritely Brown-headed Nuthatch is a classic bird of open pine woodlands, and is almost never found far from pine trees. Knowing its habitat makes it easy to find.

else, many species are dimorphic, which means the males and females carry different plumages. And more, most bird species have distinct plumages for adults and young birds. And that's before you even begin to consider variation between individuals, plumage abnormalities, including pigment issues, and the regular process of replacing worn feathers, called molt. Many species can give you many different looks over the course of a year or a lifetime, but focusing on constants like shape, habitat, and behavior will also help you to find the right species even when an individual doesn't look exactly like the photo in your field guide.

Be aware of the sounds that birds are making when you're looking for them. Not only will vocalizations clue you in on where to look, but they can be an easy way to identify birds that are not always easy to see. Rails, nightjars, and owls are notoriously difficult to find, and are mostly nocturnal, but most call loudly and frequently when present. Descriptions of vocalizations, including helpful mnemonics where appropriate, are included in the species account for many species in this

Streaky female Red-winged Blackbirds are easy to confuse for sparrows as they look very little like the glossy males, but their structure, behavior, and habitat preferences will give them away.

book. They are intended to serve as a memorization tool to help you remember what you are hearing in the field. But there is no substitute for spending time birding if you truly want to get comfortable with bird vocalizations. You can create your own mnemonic devices that are meaningful and memorable to you, if that helps. Practice makes perfect, and getting familiar with the common birds in your area is key, as that will make you better able to pick out that something different that can lead you to a new bird!

Parts of a Bird

This book avoids the use of technical terms for bird parts as much as possible, but in some cases it cannot be avoided. The following annotated photos illustrate a few important plumage and structural aspects of four major groups of birds: waterfowl, gulls, raptors, and perching birds.

PARTS OF WATERFOWL
This Ring-necked Duck, like most waterfowl, has a short tail, long low body, and large head with a deep, blunt, bill.

crown

forehead

nape

bill

back

tail

breast

side

PARTS OF A GULL
Gulls often loaf on beaches and mudflats in large mixed flocks, making comparisons between species and ages easier.

crown · iris · eye ring · back (mantle) · spot · gape · breast · wingtip · tail · leg · belly

PARTS OF A RAPTOR
Raptors are often seen in flight, and have many useful field marks on the spread wings and tail, like the black wingtips and the tail band on this male Northern Harrier.

flight feathers (primaries) · tail band · rump · wrist · back · tail · shoulder · flight feathers (secondaries)

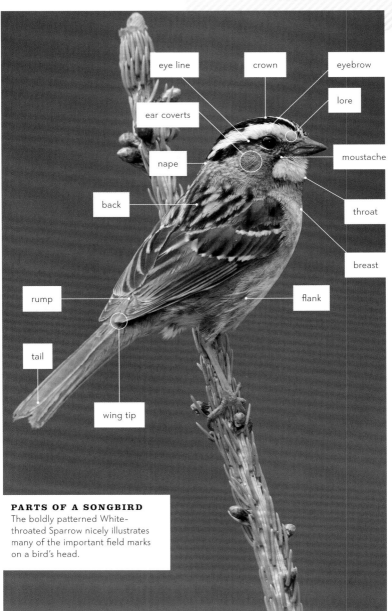

eye line

crown

eyebrow

lore

ear coverts

moustache

nape

throat

back

breast

rump

flank

tail

wing tip

PARTS OF A SONGBIRD
The boldly patterned White-
throated Sparrow nicely illustrates
many of the important field marks
on a bird's head.

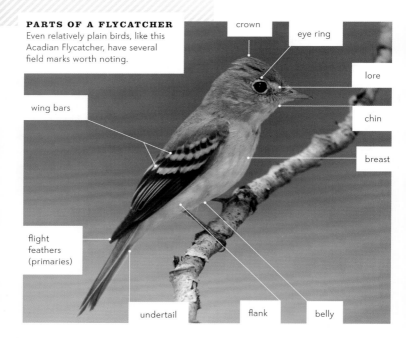

PARTS OF A FLYCATCHER
Even relatively plain birds, like this
Acadian Flycatcher, have several
field marks worth noting.

crown

eye ring

lore

wing bars

chin

breast

flight
feathers
(primaries)

undertail

flank

belly

Birding in the Carolinas

The diverse habitats of the Carolinas, and the diverse bird
populations they hold, offer abundant birding opportunities
throughout both states. A birder in North or South Carolina
does not have to go far to enjoy excellent birding.

Sites with the highest species diversity are typically found
towards the coast of both states, and the single best birding
spots in either state, according to eBird (www.ebird.org) the
popular online checklist and bird records database, lie right on
the ocean. For North Carolina, that site is Pea Island NWR, on
the Outer Banks in Dare County, with well over 300 species
recorded.

In fact, Dare County itself, which contains not only the Outer Banks and offshore waters, with exceptional seabirding, but significant onshore land area, can claim more than 400 species on its own, nearly 90 percent of the species ever recorded in North Carolina. The next four counties in terms of species richness—Carteret, New Hanover, Brunswick, and Hyde counties—also share ample coastlines, marshes, and tidal flats that attract many birds.

Wake County, which includes the city of Raleigh, arguably has the most active birding community in North Carolina, at least as determined by eBird checklists submitted. It is followed closely by Durham, Forsyth (Winston-Salem), and Mecklenburg (Charlotte).

South Carolina's brightest birding jewel is undoubtedly Huntington Beach State Park in Georgetown County, with 326 species recorded in eBird. However, the county with the highest total is Charleston County, just to the south, which claims nearly 400 species, as well as a full third of South Carolina's

The beaches and extensive sandbars along the coast of North and South Carolina offer excellent nesting sites for coastal birds like Black Skimmer.

coastline. Other coastal counties round out the top five in South Carolina. Charleston also has a very active birding community, but tops in the state is held by Spartanburg County, which lies in the foothills of the mountains.

COAST This refers to the immediate coast of the Carolinas, that land which borders the ocean from the Virginia border in the north to the Georgia border in the south. Sandy beaches, brackish tidal marshes, and ephemeral tidal flats and sandbars, often with man-made impoundments nearby.

Hotspots North Carolina Pea Island NWR, Cape Hatteras National Seashore, Cape Lookout National Seashore, Fort Fisher

Hotspots South Carolina Huntington Beach State Park, Santee Coastal Reserve, Pinckney Island NWR

The spectacular Painted Bunting is a common breeding bird in the maritime scrub of Huntington Beach State Park and other coastal sites in South Carolina.

COASTAL PLAIN The lowland area between the coast and the fall line, roughly I-95. Largely agricultural, with swamps in lowlands and pine woodlands in higher elevations.

Hotspots NC Pocosin Lakes NWR, Mattamuskeet NWR, Croatan National Forest, Holly Shelter Game Land

Hotspots SC Francis Marion National Forest, Bear Island WMA, Savannah NWR, Santee NWR

SANDHILLS A unique, and highly dynamic, habitat of the Southeast, characterized by open Longleaf Pine savannahs. Generally, in south-central NC and north-central SC.

Hotspots NC Sandhills Game Land, Weymouth Woods Sandhills Nature Preserve

Hotspots SC Sandhills NWR

PIEDMONT The highest population density in the Carolinas, located between the Coastal Plain and the mountains. Rolling hills, mixed hardwood/pine forests, and pasture.

Hotspots NC Jordan Lake, Lake Norman, Lake Crabtree Park, Eno River State Park, Pilot Mountain State Park, Uwharrie National Forest

Most of eastern North America's Tundra Swans spend the winter at refuges in North Carolina's Coastal Plain, among hundreds of thousands of other waterfowl.

Hotspots SC Lake Conestee Nature Park, Clemson-Simpson Research Station, Saluda Shoals Park, Congaree National Park

MOUNTAINS THE Southern Appalachians, often called the Blue Ridge Mountains (or just termed "mountains" in this book), throughout western NC into northwest SC. Mount Mitchell, in NC, is the highest point in eastern North America at 6,684 ft. Extensive hardwood or mixed forests, spruce-fir in highest elevations.

Hotspots NC Great Smoky Mountains National Park, Blue Ridge Parkway, Mount Mitchell State Park, Roan Mountain.

Hotspots SC Caesar's Head State Park, Sassafras Mountain, Table Rock State Park

The high mountains of the western Carolinas host species at the very southern tip of their breeding range, like Chestnut-sided Warbler.

A Year in Birding

While the Carolinas boast nearly 500 species between them, only about half of those are present at any one time of year. As the seasons change, different species come and go, requiring different strategies for making the most of your birding experiences. The following is a summary of birdlife trends over the course of the year, with suggestions for birding hotspots for each month. These hotspots represent only a few of the many places in the Carolinas where one can experience great birdwatching.

JANUARY Relatively moderate temperatures, particularly on the coast, mean that many species from farther north over-winter in the Carolinas. Waterfowl, in particular, are at their highest diversity in January and reach their greatest congregations at National Wildlife Refuges in the Coastal Plain.

FEBRUARY February is a good time to check large reservoirs for refugees from frozen water farther north. Waterfowl numbers in the eastern refuges begin to tail off by the end of the month, and early spring migrants like Louisiana Waterthrush, Purple Martin, and Blue-gray Gnatcatcher begin to trickle in. Owls call to mates at night, and American Woodcocks are displaying in boggy fields throughout the Carolinas.

MARCH Spring begins to arrive throughout the month with trees leafing out in the Coastal Plain and eastern Piedmont. Migration begins to become more evident even as the biggest push is still several weeks off. Owls and Bald Eagles are on eggs, and many species of southern breeding warblers return to their territories.

APRIL Migration really starts to happen in a big way. On the coast, protected tidal flats fill up with migrating shorebirds on their way north. Those shorebirds and terns that breed in the Carolinas have arrived and settle in colonies. Ruby-throated Hummingbirds return and take advantage of flowering buckeyes as well as sugar water feeders. Across the interior of the Carolinas, forested areas are alive with the songs of arriving migrants setting up breeding territories. By the end of the month, most every breeding bird in the Carolinas is either on territory or actively nesting.

MAY The first week of May is arguably the most exciting time for birding in the Carolinas. Most of the birds that breed in the far north of the continent are passing through en masse, mixing with resident breeders. Birding is excellent everywhere, but migration is particularly apparent in the mountains and western Piedmont. By the end of the month land migration begins to wane, but pelagic birding (birding from a boat) in the Gulf Stream can be incredibly productive.

JUNE Migration mostly comes to a halt in early summer and general activity slows, as birds are busy tending to nests or young. June can be a great time to find birds on territory, particularly those breeding in the Appalachians as the temperatures are more moderate at high elevations. Many overlooks along the Blue Ridge Parkway offer accessible views into the forest canopy.

Beach-nesting birds like Least Terns, arrive in April and quickly set up shop on sandbars and inlets up and down the coast.

JULY As breeding finishes up, the adults of many species begin to molt, and disheveled looking birds are the norm, aolng with juvenile birds, which often appear streaky and unusual. By the end of the month, shorebirds begin to return south, pausing on coastal tidal flats and the exposed mudflats of large reservoirs.

AUGUST Fall migration begins in earnest, particularly along the coast, as young shorebirds begin to arrive in numbers. Herons and egrets disperse widely after breeding and can often be found well inland on ponds and shallow arms of large reservoirs. Some southern species disperse up the coast into South Carolina and southern North Carolina. Hummingbird feeders are busy as young Ruby-throated Hummingbirds begin to feed for themselves, and northern migrants pass through on their way south.

SEPTEMBER The busiest month for fall migration across the entirety of the Carolinas as birds gradually move southward. The mountains are particularly good as songbirds follow the ridges.

Early summer is an excellent time to find breeding birds, like Canada Warbler, in the Blue Ridge Mountains.

Tropical storms in the Atlantic occasionally make landfall, pushing coastal birds inland to large reservoirs. The last week brings large numbers of migrating hawks, particularly Broad-winged Hawks in the mountains at sites like Caesar's Head State Park, and Sharp-shinned Hawks and falcons along the coast. Ruby-throated Hummingbirds begin to depart.

OCTOBER Most neotropical migrants have moved on, and cold fronts begin to pass through more regularly bringing overwintering birds. Sparrows arrive around the middle of the month, along with kinglets and masses of Yellow-rumped Warblers, the latter particularly along the coast. Scoters and loons are migrating southward in large numbers just offshore towards the end of the month. Waterfowl begins to trickle in to traditional wintering sites along the coast.

Yellow-rumped Warblers, in somber fall plumage, migrate down the coast in large numbers in October. Hundreds can often be seen in one day.

NOVEMBER Most winter residents have arrived, though a few late migrants make their way south into the Carolinas. November is an exceptional time for oddities in the Southeast, primarily vagrants from western North America. Those who have left up hummingbird feeders might be visited by a Rufous Hummingbird or another western species. Waterfowl begin to arrive in larger numbers and diversity. Gulls flocks along the coast get larger and more diverse, and Northern Gannets are common just offshore.

DECEMBER Waterfowl continues to arrive into December, particularly diving ducks. The first cold snaps of the year concentrate birds at sites that offer food and shelter, like large bodies of water or feeding stations. Moderate temperatures near the coast may allow for some lingering migrants to stick it out for several weeks, or even the entire winter in warmer years.

Northern Pintail is one of the more common overwintering duck species in the Carolinas, and arrives in large numbers mostly in November.

Additional Resources

This book is intended to provide an overview of the birds and birding opportunities in the Carolinas, but interested birders can find a great many additional resources to further their knowledge.

ONLINE RESOURCES

The Carolinabirds email group (https://lists.duke.edu/sympa/info/carolinabirds) is perhaps the most notable tool for communication among birders in North and South Carolina. It provides a forum for discussion about wild birds and birding throughout both states. Questions, discussions about status and distribution, and reports of rare and notable species are all par for the course.

The well-regarded Cornell Lab of Ornithology (allaboutbirds.org) offers a website that includes summaries of the natural history, behavior, and status and distribution of most bird species found in the United States and Canada. It also includes a comprehensive library of vocalizations of North American birds.

eBird (http://ebird.org) is an online crowd-sourced checklist for recording your own bird sightings, as well as a comprehensive, searchable database for exploring the sightings of other birders. It is impossible to overstate the usefulness of the site. Not only can you explore real-time maps of species distribution and seasonal abundance, but you can use eBird to explore places to bird near your home, as well as sites to find species you'd like to see anywhere in the world.

Birders in North Carolina can find a state-specific database at Birds of NC (http://ncbirds.carolinabirdclub.org/), created by Harry LeGrand and others. The site includes every species recorded in the state, including status and distribution, seasonal abundance, maps of occurrence by county, and general information for locating the species when appropriate. Because it is online, it is regularly updated with new information as needed.

BOOKS

This book contains most species you are likely to encounter in the Carolinas, but for those species that are not included, a good field guide to the entirety of the US and Canada is useful. Good options include *The Sibley Guide to Birds*, second edition (Knopf, 2014) by David Sibley for those who like illustrations or the *Smithsonian Field Guide to Birds of North America* (HarperCollins, 2008) by Ted Floyd, if you prefer photos.

Birders in the Carolinas may also be interested in useful bird-finding guides. The late Robin Carter's *Finding Birds in South Carolina* (University of South Carolina Press, 1993) is a little dated but still extremely useful for birding the Palmetto State. It is available for free via the Carolina Bird Club (https://www.carolinabirdclub.org/sites/SC/FindingBirdsInSouthCarolina.pdf).

Marcus Simpson's *Birds of the Blue Ridge Mountains* (University of North Carolina Press, 1992) and John Fussell's *A Birder's Guide to Coastal North Carolina* (University of North Carolina Press, 1994) are comprehensive guides to birding sites in their respective regions that hold up remarkably well despite being more than 20 years old. The latter consists only of NC sites, while the former includes both western South Carolina and Virginia, as well.

BIRD CLUBS

The birding community in the Carolinas is friendly, knowledge-able, and quite active. Most all of the major urban centers across both states host local Audubon chapters or bird clubs that offer regular birding field trips, guided walks, and social meetings. There a great many people with whom you can share your interest, and who are more than happy to share their knowledge about birding in North and South Carolina.

The Carolina Bird Club (www.carolinabirdclub.org) is a good place to start. The CBC welcomes birders of all skill levels and experience, and supports the birding community of the Carolinas with regular meetings held three times annually in various spots around the Carolinas. Members also receive an excellent quarterly publication, *The Chat*.

The American Birding Association (ABA) represent birders in the United States and Canada, and advocates for birding and birder interests throughout. Members are not only plugged into a continental birding community, but they receive excellent publications throughout the year, and various other benefits. Information about the ABA can be found at www.aba.org.

American Birding Association

Field Guide to Birds
of the Carolinas

Black-bellied Whistling Duck

Dendrocygna autumnalis

L 19″ | **WS** 36″

The dramatic and unmistakable Black-bellied Whistling-Duck was introduced into South Carolina, where it is now established as a breeder along the southern coast of the state and an increasing stray to elsewhere in the Carolinas. More terrestrial than most ducks, it can often be seen perched on snags or on half-submerged logs or grazing in short grass. In flight, shows a flashy white wing stripe. Can be found most reliably at Savannah NWR and Donnelly Wildlife Management Area south of Charleston, South Carolina, but increasing up the coast as far north as southern North Carolina. Call is a wheezy whistle, which is how the bird gets its name.

Like a cross between a goose and a duck, and strikingly patterned in black and chestnut. Note bright red bill (gray in young birds) and long pink legs.

Snow Goose

Chen caerulescens

L 30″ | **WS** 54″

The combination of eggshell plumage, black wingtips, and orange-red bill is unique among all native North American waterfowl. From October until March, many thousands of this medium-sized goose funnel into refuges in eastern North Carolina, notably Pocosin Lakes, Mattamuskeet, and Pea Island. Less common in South Carolina, but many overwinter at Santee NWR. Outside of those refuges in the east, Snow Goose is an uncommon winter visitor across both Carolinas, often mixed in with flocks of Canada Geese, where it is conspicuous when present. Most birds in the Carolinas are "white morph" birds. Flocks are raucous; call is a brassy *henk*.

Stocky, brightly-colored bill with broad black "lips." Young birds often dingy gray, with gray-pink bill and legs.

In flight, note heavy body, broad wings with black tips; white domestic geese usually lack black in wing.

Ross's Goose

Chen rossii

L 23″ | **WS** 45″

In all aspects, very much like a plush-toy version of Snow Goose. Massive flocks of Snow Geese at eastern North Carolina refuges typically hold up to a dozen of these small geese every year, fairly easily picked out given a good look at a flock. Uncommon, but seems to be increasing, elsewhere in the Carolinas.

Similar to Snow Goose, but smaller. Note rounded head with more centered eye, tiny bill with limited black, and more pristine white plumage.

Cackling Goose

Branta hutchinsii

L 25″ | **WS** 51″

A miniature version of Canada Goose, often not much larger than large ducks. Can be found annually among flocks of Snow Geese on eastern North Carolina refuges. They are still quite rare in South Carolina.

Like a Canada Goose stuck in the dryer too long; note small bill, rounded head, and compact impression.

Brant
Branta bernicla

L 25″ | **WS** 45″

A stout-bodied sea goose, formerly present in great numbers along the Outer Banks from Oregon Inlet to Ocracoke Island in North Carolina from October through April, but no longer as reliable as in the past. Likely still present in numbers in the Pamlico Sound, but out of sight of birders on land. Still locally common in some places, as wintering populations often stop short of the Carolinas to overwinter in states to the north, where eelgrass, their preferred food, is more prevalent. Casual in coastal South Carolina and inland.

Appears dark, small-billed at distance, with obvious patch of white around the tail. White collar around neck variable, not often seen from far away. Flies in fast-moving, messy lines, often just off the water. Wings more pointed than other geese.

Canada Goose
Branta canadensis

L 30–43" | **WS** 50–67"

The ubiquitous "golf course goose" is well-known to birders and non-birders alike, and semi-feral birds can be found across both states wherever there's a small pond and a grassy lawn. Migratory populations of Canada Geese breed in the Arctic and migrate south to overwinter on the Albermarle Peninsula of eastern North Carolina and along the shores of Pamlico Sound. They are smaller bodied, with shorter necks and bills, than the resident birds elsewhere, and can be found in flocks of dozens to hundreds at many of the eastern wildlife refuges. Call is a familiar resonant *hhh-NONK*.

Shuttles from roosting sites to feeding sites in loose flocks. Often, but not always, in familiar V formation. Large and dark, with long, broad wings.

Large-bodied and large-billed, with familiar black head and neck and white cheek.

Mute Swan

Cygnus olor

L 60″ | **WS** 75″

The massive, all-white Mute Swan was introduced to North America from Europe. Feral birds nest across both states, but most individuals in the Carolinas are of recent domestic origin and are not often seen far from human habitation. Individuals in the northeast corner of North Carolina could potentially come from established populations in the Chesapeake Bay region, but culling operations to the north have contributed to a decline in birds there. In recent years these semi-feral birds have become harder to find. True to their name, Mute Swans are mostly silent, though they can hiss when disturbed.

Exceptionally large with entirely white plumage. Coral-colored bill is unlike any native swan. At rest, neck has a slight curve.

Tundra Swan

Cygnus columbianus

L 52″ | **WS** 66″

Small by swan standards but still larger than all but a couple of species of waterfowl, Tundra Swan is an iconic species of eastern North Carolina. A significant percentage of the Atlantic population winters in the state, and thousands can be found on refuges like Alligator River, Mattamuskeet, Pocosin Lakes, and Pea Island, lounging on impoundments and feeding during the day in fallow agricultural fields. They are less common in South Carolina, but several dozen usually winter at Bear Island Wildlife Management Area and Santee Coastal Reserve near Charleston. They are scarce in the Piedmont and mountains. Call is a high-pitched resonant *hoot*, and large flocks calling together have a pleasant musical quality.

Large and unmistakable, often holds neck straight like a flagpole. Bill black with a small yellow spot near the eye. Young birds dingy, with varying pink in the bill.

Wood Duck

Aix sponsa

L 20″ | **WS** 27″

Few birds in North America inspire as much awe as a well-seen male Wood Duck. Its kaleidoscopic plumage makes it hard to mistake for any other native waterfowl. Wood Duck is a common sight across both states in tree-lined ponds, flooded hardwood forests, and swampy bottomlands. Cavity nesters, Wood Ducks take readily to nest boxes, and the wide distribution of those boxes has contributed to an impressive increase in their numbers from a low in the 1900s. Call is a shrill rising squeal, most often heard when birds are flushed from wooded ponds or swamps.

Male is impossibly gorgeous: technicolor bill, crested green head with white streaks, chestnut breast, buff sides, and long tail. In late summer plumage, colors are gone but head pattern mostly remains.

Female more subdued, plain brown with white speckling. Eye surrounded by white teardrop.

Gadwall

Anas strepera

L 20″ | **WS** 33″

The subdued, square-headed Gadwall is a common winter dabbling duck across both states on both salt and freshwater. Can be found wintering in the hundreds at places where waterfowl congregate along the coast, like Pea Island, Alligator River, or Mattamuskeet in North Carolina and Huntington Beach State Park, Cape Romain NWR, and Santee NWR in South Carolina. Usually present in smaller numbers on millponds, impoundments, and reservoirs elsewhere. Small numbers of Gadwall have been recorded nesting in brackish marshes in the northeast corner of North Carolina. Call is a burpy, thin quack often paired with a squeaky *peep*, a common component of the waterfowl chorus at large refuges.

Male subtle and gray, with fine marbled patterns when seen well. Head is bulky and squarish; black bill and black rear-end. In flight, shows large white square on the hind wing.

Female fairly plain, but with squarish head. Bill mostly black but with orange edges.

Eurasian Wigeon

Anas penelope

L 18" | **WS** 32"

Compact and rotund, this European visitor can predictably
be found among large flocks of wintering waterfowl along
the coast every year. Practically all reports of the species in
the Carolinas are of the handsome rufous-headed male, as the
female is virtually identical to the female American Wigeon and
likely goes overlooked. Places where Eurasian Wigeon is found
annually include Mattamuskeet and Pea Island NWRs in North
Carolina and Cape Romain NWR and Santee Coastal Reserve
in South Carolina. Birders can be rewarded by looking closely
through flocks of ducks for the one with the copper head.

Copper-penny head with buff forehead
unlike any North American dabbling duck.
Body is mostly paler gray and contrasting,
rear is black. Females nearly identical to
American Wigeon.

American Wigeon

Anas americana

L 20" | **WS** 32"

The round-headed, short-billed American Wigeon has a distribution similar to most ducks in the Carolinas. A mostly winter resident with concentrations of hundreds found towards the coast, dozens in the Piedmont, and singles and small groups in the mountains. This handsome duck can be found both on freshwater and and on sheltered saltwater coves. It is one of the more common dabblers on the eastern refuges in both states, particularly at Mattamuskeet and Pea Island in NC and Savannah and Santee in SC. Their constant wheezing *ZHEE-zhee-zer* is hard to miss in mixed flocks.

Male is cute, with rounded head and small grayish bill. Pale forehead contrasts with shimmery green eye stripe and darker rusty body. In flight, shows a square white patch on the forewing.

Female with dainty proportions; round head is pale with dark smudges around the eye.

American Black Duck

Anas rubripes

L 23" | **WS** 35"

Large, long, and dark, the American Black Duck was formerly a common breeding bird in the brackish marshes of northeast North Carolina and the Outer Banks. Those breeders have declined in recent years, in part due to an increasing population of resident Mallards squeezing them out, but the species is still a fairly common wintering bird across the rest of the Carolinas. Black Ducks prefer salt water more than most other dabbling duck species, and are frequently found on calm coastal bays and sounds. Elsewhere, any body of water of decent size is likely to attract them between October and April. Close study of any flock of American Black Ducks is likely to reveal birds with various Mallard features, as hybrids between the two closely related species are regular. Voice is a familiar *QUACK*, very similar to that of Mallard.

Both sexes mostly rich dark brown, appearing black at a distance, with a paler head. Males have a yellow to green-yellow bill, females more dingy. Heavy-bodied in flight, with long head and bill. Wing patch deep blue, often appearing purple, with no white borders. Underwing flashes white.

Mottled Duck

Anas fulvigula

L 20″ | **WS** 34″

One of the few resident breeding ducks in the Carolinas, Mottled Duck was introduced to South Carolina decades ago as hunting quarry. It has since established a robust breeding population on the coast, and has wandered as far north as southern North Carolina in recent years. Unlike the similar Mallard and American Black Duck, Mottled Duck tends not to flock and is frequently seen singly or in pairs. They favor freshwater, particularly old rice plantations and natural marshes. Reliable spots include the Wildlife Management Areas and NWRs in southern South Carolina, particularly Bear Island WMA, Savannah Spoil Area, and Santee Coastal Reserve. Vocalizations are similar to Mallard but less coarse.

Similar to female Mallard, but note clean buffy throat, boldly patterned body feathers, and black spot at the base of the bill.

In flight, entire upperside of wing is dark. Blue patch on hindwing lacks white borders seen in Mallard.

Mallard
Anas platyrhynchos

L 23" | **WS** 35"

The familiar green-headed male Mallard is the prototypical duck for many birders and non-birders. Formerly only a wintering bird in the Carolinas, the proliferation of semi-feral "park ducks" across the continent makes determining the origins of any individual bird nearly impossible. Such birds vary widely in plumage, and those with a multitude of colors and patterns are often found mixed with "wild-type" Mallards on any body of water in either state. Undeniably wild birds spend the winter on the coasts of both states among large flocks of waterfowl, and are generally warier than birds found elsewhere. Vocalizations include a familiar *QUACK*, and females often give a coarse, descending laugh.

Male with glowing green head, appears dark in poor light. Yellow bill, chestnut breast, and gray body.

Female plain, mottled brown with paler head. Bill large, mostly orange with black smudges.

Blue-winged Teal

Anas discors

L 15″ | **WS** 23″

Unlike most ducks in this book, the lithe little Blue-winged Teal is most common in spring and fall migration, as most of the population winters to the south of the Carolinas. A few linger through the winter on freshwater impoundments near the coast, particularly in the south of South Carolina, but the vast majority of the birds are seen in March and April in the spring and from August to November in the fall. Like most dabbling ducks, Blue-wing Teals prefer impoundments and small ponds, particularly those with marshy edges, and almost always freshwater. Mostly silent, but males make high-pitched whistled *peeps*.

Slender with fairly large black bill, male with flashy white crescent on the blue-gray face, subtly patterned body. White patch on the hip and black tail.

Female mostly gray-brown, with subtle scalloping on back and sides. Usually some white on the face. Bill black and broad.

Northern Shoveler

Anas clypeata

L 19" | **WS** 30"

A middle-sized duck with an enormous spoon-shaped bill, the silhouette of Northern Shoveler is immediately distinctive even at great distance. Like several other dabbling ducks, it is common to abundant in winter at refuges in the lower Coastal Plain of both states, including Mattamuskeet and Pea Island NWRs in North Carolina and Savannah and Santee NWRs in South Carolina. Apparently increasing in recent decades inland, it is a fairly common winter visitor at various reservoirs and impoundments west of the Coastal Plain. It frequents smaller bodies of water than many other dabblers, and can be found on farm ponds and residential lakes across both states except at very high elevations. Mostly silent, but males make a guttural *THUCK-a*.

Enormous bill unmistakable in all plumages. Male with piercing yellow eye on dark green head, white breast and chestnut sides. Female mostly buffy all over, with orangey bill.

Bill massive in flight. Males show extensive pale blue in forewing, green in hindwing. Female similar but grayish instead of blue.

Northern Pintail

Anas acuta

L 25″ | **WS** 34″

The svelte Northern Pintail is often referred to as the "grey-hound of the air" because of its long and lean appearance. Like other dabbling ducks, it gathers in the thousands in eastern North Carolina at Mattamuskeet, Alligator River, and Pea Island NWRs, and in smaller numbers elsewhere along the coast and inland in both Carolinas. Pintails prefer larger bodies of water, reservoirs and impoundments, and will even gather on shallow saltwater bays, where flocks can often be found holding court out on the open water. Their longer necks allow them to feed at greater depths, tipping forward and displaying the long whip of a tail in the air. Mostly silent, but males can sometimes be heard displaying in late winter with a buzzy *zzzzzzzzzz* followed by a hollow *PEEP*.

Males with whip tail and long, slender neck. Elegant gray body, white breast, and brown head.

Female structure like male, plumage buffy and plain, particularly the head.

Wings longer and more pointed than other dabbling ducks.

Green-winged Teal

Anas crecca

L 14″ | **WS** 23″

The compact, short-billed Green-winged Teal is the smallest of North America's duck species, a fact that is readily apparent in large mixed flocks of wintering waterfowl. Even in flight, their compact wheeling flocks with buzzy wingbeats are hard to mistake for any other species. Can number in hundreds or thousands at refuges in the eastern part of North Carolina in winter, less abundant but still common elsewhere on the coast. An uncommon wintering duck inland, where mostly seen at reservoirs and ponds in migration. Fond of mudflats in fall, and can be seen walking around like an overweight shorebird. Males make a high-pitched *prreet-prreet* not unlike a frog or cricket.

Compact and dark overall. Male has dashing head pattern and white spur at the shoulder.

Female mostly plain and dark, with rounded head and smallish bill.

Small, with whirring wingbeats. Body and head short and round, and neck not appreciably thinner.

Canvasback
Aythya valisineria
L 21″ | **WS** 33″

Although the least common of the overwintering diving ducks in the Carolinas, the elegant Canvasback can still be found reliably at a few sites along the coast. Their stay is brief, arriving later than most waterfowl in mid- to late November and mostly leaving by mid-March. Lake Phelps in eastern North Carolina is perhaps the most consistent spot in either state for the species, but they can also be found in sheltered bays along the entire coast, sometimes in good numbers. In colder winters they move into the Piedmont, and the deeper portions of larger reservoirs, such as Jordan Lake and Lake Norman in NC and Lake Marion in SC, sometimes harbor small flocks.

Two-toned "Oreo" body, dark on the ends and white in the middle. Head appears mostly dark with long, sloping forehead and all-black bill.

Female shaped like male, with peaked head and long, sloping forehead and black bill. Mostly sandy brown on head and breast, pale gray elsewhere.

Redhead
Aythya americana

L 19" | **WS** 29"

Appropriately named, the Redhead is an attractive but uncommon and highly localized winter resident. Distribution is spotty across much of the Carolinas for this classic "bay duck," and larger reservoirs can host small flocks that never seem to stick around for long. It occurs in dense single-species flocks numbering in the thousands on Pamlico Sound and at Pea Island NWR, in North Carolina, and these numbers seem to be increasing in recent years. Flocks look like an oil slick at a distance, and only through a scope does one see the churning mass of ducks within.

Rounded head is bright rufous; body slate gray bounded by black on breast and tail, appears very dark. Bill is blue with a black tip.

Female a uniform dingy brown, bill black. Rounded head and back.

Ring-necked Duck

Aythya collaris

L 17" | **WS** 25"

Ring-necked Duck is an unfortunate name for this peak-headed diver. Males do have a faint chestnut band around the neck, but it's almost never seen in the field. It is a common winter resident on all freshwater bodies of water in the Carolinas, from large reservoirs to small ponds in the suburbs. Unlike other diving ducks, they mostly eschew open water for the tree-lined edges. Wintering populations seem to be on the rise in the Carolinas due to an increase in reservoirs, beaver ponds, and retention ponds in recent decades.

Conehead profile, peaked towards the back. Bill dark with obvious white band towards the tip. Male has entirely black back, sides gray with white spur at the shoulder.

Female mostly gray-brown all over, same peak-headed profile and banded bill. Variable amount of white on the face and around the eye.

Bufflehead

Bucephala albeola

L 13″ | **WS** 21″

Diminutive and cute, the Bufflehead is a common to locally abundant winter resident in nearly all flat-water habitats, both salt and fresh. This active little duck with the too-big head is present in the Carolinas from November to April. Tends not to congregate in tight flocks as other diving ducks do, and scatters widely across the water even in places where many occur. Pair-bonding occurs on wintering grounds, so it's not uncommon for Carolina birders to see animated Bufflehead drakes head-bobbing and flapping to a chorus of high-pitched cackles in an attempt to win a mate.

Short-bodied and large-headed, and bill seems stubby. Male with quarter-circle patch of white on the back of puffy, mostly dark head. Back black; breast, sides, and tail white.

Female mostly dark gray, with large white patch near the ear.

Greater Scaup
Aythya marila

L 18" | **WS** 28"

The slightly larger and slightly less common of the two Oreo-patterned scaup species, both of which are regular wintering birds in the Carolinas. Greater Scaup tends to prefer saltwater environments where it can form large rafts on sheltered bays, sounds, or nearshore waters, but can be locally common at some inland sites, generally reservoirs with significant expanses of open water.

Fairly compact, male with whitish body with black breast and tail. Head is large and round, peaked towards the forehead. Broad bill has wide black spot at the tip. Head of male may show greenish cast.

Female mostly brown all over, structurally like male with rounded head peaked towards the front, broad bill with wide black tip. White patch on the face tends to be crisply demarcated, often shows a little white around the ear.

Lesser Scaup

Aythya affinis

L 16″ | **WS** 29″

Slightly smaller and generally more common throughout the Carolinas than Greater Scaup. The peak-headed Lesser Scaup is more often found at freshwater sites, traditionally large reservoirs and impoundments close to the coast, less common the farther one travels inland. It is sporadically found in protected bays and sounds as well, particularly in South Carolina, where it forms large rafts on nearshore waters.

Male has pale gray back and sides, black breast and tail. Best identified by head shape, peaked towards the back of the head and eye more centered. Bill blue, slender, with limited black tip. Head tends to show purplish cast, but occasionally green.

Female chocolate brown all over. Head shape distinctive, more peaked than rounded. White on face tends to be dirtier and less cleanly demarcated.

Surf Scoter
Melanitta perspicillata

L 23″ | **WS** 30″

The clown-faced Surf Scoter is a common sea duck in both Carolinas, but particularly so off the northern beaches of North Carolina. Mixed flocks of scoters, typically containing several Surf Scoters, are a regular sight from shore from October through March. Readily flocks with Black Scoters, and birders should check flocks of scoters for birds with the white patches and a huge "nose." Large concentrations of these birds gather in Pamlico Sound every year, but are usually only viewable by boat. The car ferry from Swan Quarter to Ocracoke Island can be a great platform from which to observe them. Young birds occasionally turn up on inland reservoirs in winter.

Heavy-set, long-bodied, all dark. Male has large colorful bill shaped like a triangle and a goofy expression. White spots on forehead and nape obvious even when the face is hidden.

Females and young birds of both sexes similar, with dark gray body, too-large head with triangle bill and black cap. Two white patches on the face, at the base of the bill and near the ear.

White-winged Scoter

Melanitta fusca

L 21" | **WS** 31"

Generally the least common scoter in the Carolinas, the heavily built White-winged Scoter has a spotty distribution along the coast. It's most common along the Outer Banks, becoming less so as you travel south. Less apt to form flocks than the other sea ducks, birders usually find them singly or in pairs. While it's the least common scoter on the coast, it's generally the most likely to show up on inland reservoirs. Their presence in the Carolinas is largely correlated with the freezing of lakes to the north.

Black, heavy-bodied and long, with a large head and long bill. Small white comma around eye. Typically shows a little sliver of the white wing patch at rest, much more obvious in flight.

Female wholly dark brownish-gray. Heavy-bodied and long. Steep forehead with slender bill. Two largish white spots on the face, at the lore and at the ear.

Black Scoter

Melanitta americana

L 19″ | **WS** 33″

A common and at times abundant wintering sea duck in the Carolinas, the cute Black Scoter is the easiest of the three species of scoters to find in either state. In October, impressive flights of Black Scoters stream past the Outer Banks heading south. It is the most common scoter seen from beaches in southern North Carolina and in South Carolina, where it winters in large flocks offshore. Readily congregates with Surf Scoter in mixed flocks. The least likely of the scoters to be found inland.

The most traditionally "ducky" of the sea ducks. Both sexes compact and round-headed with relatively short bills. Male shiny black with a bright orange bulb at the base of the bill.

Female pale gray with a black cap and a white cheek.

Long-tailed Duck
Clangula hyemalis

L 15-23″ | **WS** 28″

In behavior and distribution, the piebald Long-tailed Duck is more or less a small scoter. Uncommon and local in brackish and salt water, most birds in the Carolinas winter on the Pamlico Sound. Birders crossing on the ferry from Swan Quarter to Ocracoke Island often find a few in waters close to the mainland. Elsewhere along the coast it's far less reliable, but can be found near marinas and breakwaters anywhere in the Carolinas. A rare visitor to inland lakes in winter. The most vocal sea duck, its call is a rich four-part yelp that gives it the colloquial name "Tom Connolly."

Compact with round head. Male dashing in white with black highlights. Black and pink bill and long black tail unmistakable.

Female and young birds similar. More subdued, compact, mostly white with smudgy gray and black marks.

Common Goldeneye

Bucephala clangula

L 24" | **WS** 33"

This handsome duck with a triangular head and piercing yellow eye is an uncommon and local winter resident, and can be easily missed. They are most often seen on either side of the Carolinas, regular only on large reservoirs in the mountains on North Carolina and at a couple of spots along the coast. A few typically overwinter in the Lower Cape Fear River near Fort Fisher, in North Carolina, and at Huntington Beach State Park in South Carolina. When cold weather freezes the water to the north, they can be seen more frequently at large reservoirs in the Piedmont region.

Long-bodied and low in the water. Male is mostly white with black highlights on the body. Triangular head dark, greenish in good light, with round white spot between the yellow eye and black bill.

Female with deep gray body and brownish head. Looks perpetually startled with bright yellow eye. Sliver of white in the wing sometimes apparent.

Hooded Merganser
Lophodytes cucullatus

L 18″ | **WS** 24″

This smart little duck with the massive crest is a common winter resident and sporadic breeder across both Carolinas. Like Wood Duck, it's a cavity nester and will readily use boxes constructed for that species, with the two occasionally nesting in close proximity. Unlike the other diving ducks, it prefers freshwater almost exclusively. It can be found even on relatively small bodies of water, where it feeds on small fish, tadpoles, and aquatic invertebrates. In late winter, can often be seen engaged in pair-bonding, in which males flash their crests and throw their heads back dramatically while making weird popping and growling sounds.

Small and compact. Long tail often raised. Male's crest white with black border, can be raised or lowered at will. Body mostly dark, with rufous sides and white breast. Black bill long and slender.

Female with various shades of brown, darker on back and paler on chest. Bill yellowish. Crest reddish-brown. Like an arrow in flight, with quick wingbeats.

Common Merganser

Mergus merganser

L 25" | **WS** 34"

The Carolinas lie at the very southern edge of the wintering range of the long-bodied Common Merganser. Its presence is highly local; several can usually be found wintering on Lake Phelps in eastern North Carolina, and in very cold winters a few may turn up on large, deep reservoirs elsewhere. Less common farther south, and mostly coastal in South Carolina when it occurs at all. It has been recorded breeding in recent years in western North Carolina.

Long-bodied, sits fairly high in the water. Male almost entirely white on the body, with dark, uncrested, oval head. Reddish bill thick at the base.

Female has gray body, reddish head with short crest. Crisp white chin with clean demarcation at the edges.

Red-breasted Merganser

Mergus serrator

L 27″ | **WS** 30″

The needle-billed sea duck with the punk rock hairdo is the most common wintering waterfowl species on salt water in either state. Hard to miss anywhere on the coast from November through April, when flocks can be seen feeding or loafing offshore or in protected bays. Easy to find anywhere along the Outer Banks and around Fort Fisher in North Carolina, Huntington Beach or Folly Beach in South Carolina. In fall or spring, small flocks may briefly stop over on larger lakes and reservoirs.

Both sexes long-bodied, sit very low in the water. Long bill, skinny for the entire length. Male with grayish sides, dark breast and back. Dark green head with very shaggy, unkempt crest.

Female with gray body, reddish head, ragged crest, and messy face and throat.

Ruddy Duck

Oxyura jamaicensis

L 15″ | **WS** 23″

The rotund Ruddy Duck, with its large swooping bill and cocked tail, is a common wintering duck in both states. Tight flocks of Ruddies, often with their tails flipped up, are a regular sight at impoundments, reservoirs, and fair-sized ponds throughout the Carolinas. Unlike the rest of our wintering waterfowl, Ruddy Ducks acquire their flashy breeding plumage in spring, mostly after the majority of our wintering population has left in April, so Carolina birders rarely get to see it.

Fairly small and compact, with a round head and a large swooping bill. Black-billed winter males have gray-brown body, dark cap, and large white cheek.

Long tail often cocked at a jaunty angle. Females dark brown all over, paler towards the front; head with dark cheek stripe.

Northern Bobwhite

Colinus virginianus

L 10″ | **WS** 13″

Once one of the most abundant birds in the Southeast, the chubby little Northern Bobwhite has declined precipitously in recent decades, particularly in the Piedmont. A year-round resident, it can be found most reliably in the Coastal Plain and in the Sandhills, where it prefers overgrown fields, open woods, and young clearcuts. In the winter, gathers in fairly large flocks that flush explosively from dense grasses. More often heard than seen, its assertive *whop-WHEET*, approximating its name, is a familiar part of the spring chorus in the rural parts of the Carolinas.

Plump, small-headed and short-tailed. Male with neat head pattern, white cheek and brow and black eye stripe. Finely patterned back and breast rufous with white spots.

Female similar to male, but pattern on body and head less distinct, white replaced with sandy brown.

Ruffed Grouse

Bonasa umbellus

L 17″ | **WS** 22″

Fairly common but secretive, the chicken-like Ruffed Grouse is a permanent resident of Appalachian North Carolina. It favors extensive, often young or middle-aged, hardwood forests at elevations above 2,500 feet. Most easily detected by sound in early spring when males "drum"; the soft, accelerating thump of wingbeats can carry for quite a distance. Females with chicks can be conspicuous in summer. Finding this bird is typically a matter of spending enough time in its range, and early morning drives along the Blue Ridge Parkway or any little-used road or trail in the high country are probably the best bet. Less widespread in South Carolina, known mostly from Caesar's Head and Sassafras Mountain in the far west.

Chicken-sized, finely patterned, with a little crest. Darker patches on the neck, sides barred, tail with a broad black band.

Wild Turkey
Meleagris gallopavo

L 37–46" │ **WS** 50–64"

The dinosaurian Wild Turkey was once hunted to near extirpation across the East, but has rebounded in remarkable fashion thanks to releases from captive stock. It's now a fairly common permanent resident across the Carolinas, particularly in bottomland hardwood forests along the Coastal Plain, but apparently increasing everywhere. Large-bodied with a tiny head, it takes well to pastures, fields, and parks, particularly near forest cover, often striding about imperiously in flocks of a dozen or more. While mostly terrestrial, turkeys are powerful flyers and roost at night in trees. In spring, displaying males ball up and spread their tail in an impressive display, calling a familiar and far-reaching gobble. Other vocalizations heard from flocks include various cackles and barks.

Heavy oval body, long tail and legs, relatively small naked head. Male (top) is impressive, glossy greens and browns. Female (bottom) similar to male but smaller, less glossy overall, head more feathered.

Red-throated Loon

Gavia stellata

L 25″ | **WS** 43″

The smaller of the two regularly occurring loon species in the Carolinas, the slender and pale Red-throated Loon is very common on the coast between November and April. Often seen in flight, which is fast and direct, with mostly white head often drooped below the body giving a hunchbacked appearance. Good numbers can be found at Wrightsville Beach or anywhere along the Outer Banks in North Carolina or at Huntington Beach or Edisto Beach in South Carolina, but a regular sight anywhere on the ocean. Rare visitor to deep inland reservoirs, usually in migration.

Pale gray all over, back speckled with white dots. Extensive white on face and neck, narrow gray bill appearing slightly turned up.

Common Loon

Gavia immer

L 32" | **WS** 46"

Heavy-bodied and block-headed, the Common Loon is a classic bird of northern lakes. Birders in the Carolinas typically know it as an uncommon to locally common winter visitor to deep reservoirs and nearshore waters throughout both states. It is more solitary than Red-throated Loon and less apt to form loose congregations, but more widespread, particularly inland. In flight, Common Loon is long but bulky, with a dark head and long feet trailing behind. Voice is a weird tremulous yodel, occasionally heard in the winter months and often in early spring as loons congregate to head northward.

Long and dark on the water, smudgy black and gray on head with white wedge on neck. Bill thick and gray, held horizontally. Birds in late spring often show messy version of breeding plumage. Checkerboard back, black head and bill, white stripes on neck.

Pied-billed Grebe

Podilymbus podiceps

L 13″ | **WS** 21″

The plain, stout Pied-billed Grebe is often mistaken for a duck by novice birders, but the short, tailless body and spade-shaped head are quite different from any waterfowl. Mostly a winter resident across both states, Pied-billed Grebes can be found singly or in small, loose groups on just about any body of open water from small farm ponds to large reservoirs. Generally avoids salt water but can be found in brackish marshes along the coast. Call, infrequently heard in the Carolinas, is an accelerating *hoo-hoo-hoo-HAop-HAop-HAop*.

Short, stocky body, uniformly brown, and relatively large spade-shaped head. Bill short and thick, pale gray or yellow in winter. Appears tailless.

Breeding birds have clean horn-colored bill with thick black band, black throat.

Horned Grebe

Podiceps auritus

L 14" **WS** 23"

Narrow-billed and long-necked, the Horned Grebe is fairly common from November to April on larger expanses of open water in both Carolinas. Showing no preference for salt or freshwater, they are as likely to be found on a large inland reservoir as they are in nearshore waves. They are most often seen on their own but occasionally form loose flocks of up to a dozen. Carolina birders are most familiar with the sharply bicolored winter plumage, but in spring, molting birds become irregularly mottled.

Winter birds with mostly black bodies, slender neck and head with flat crown. Sharply bicolored face. Bill slender and pale. Individuals transitioning into breeding plumage in late winter are extremely variable. Neck often mottled with rufous and face with scattered black feathers. Note flat-crowned head and slender bill.

Pelagic Species

One of the great joys of birding in the Carolinas is its proximity to the Gulf Stream, a surging river of warm water 20 to 40 miles off the beach. Strong, persistent easterly winds in the spring sometimes bring pelagic species—birds that live most of their lives on the open ocean—close enough to shore for birders to see them from land. The Outer Banks generally offers the best opportunities to see these birds. Long-winged, dark Sooty Shearwaters and paler Cory's or Great Shearwaters are the most commonly seen, often still at fair distance. This dynamic pelagic ecosystem, full of tubenoses and tropicbirds, can't be fully appreciated from shore, however. It requires a trip on a boat, often from Hatteras, North Carolina, to truly experience it.

The smoky, long-winged Sooty Shearwater (*Puffinus griseus*) is occasionally seen from shore following east winds, hanging around inlets on the Outer Banks.

Large and lazy, the yellow-billed Cory's Shearwater (*Calonectris borealis*) is the most common white-bellied shearwater seen from the beaches of eastern North Carolina.

Striking fear into seabirds, gulls, and terns, the predatory Parasitic Jaeger (*Stercorarius parasiticus*) sometimes chases its quarry within sight of shore to steal food. Dark wings and powerful wingbeats differentiate jaegers from gulls.

Northern Gannet

Morus bassanus

L 37″ | **WS** 69″

Winter on the coast always includes the thrill of watching dozens of Northern Gannets plunge diving like white missiles into the surf. This large seabird breeds in the North Atlantic, but can be seen in nearshore waters in either Carolina from October through April, with young birds sometimes lingering through the summer. Good spots for gannets include the Outer Banks and Wrightsville Beach in North Carolina, or Huntington Beach and Folly Beach in South Carolina, but they can be found in season at just about any beach in either state.

Adult (top) is mostly white with black wingtips, gray bill, wash of yellow on the head. Head and tail long and pointed like wings, giving impression of a flying plus-sign. Younger birds (right) range in color and pattern from all gray-brown juveniles to white and every pattern in between.

Anhinga
Anhinga anhinga

L 35 | **WS** 45"

The strange, long-tailed, long-necked Anhinga is a common summer resident in the Coastal Plain into southern North Carolina, preferring freshwater vegetated ponds and slow-moving swampy rivers. Swims with body submerged and only serpent-like head and bill visible above the water, whence it gets its nickname, "snakebird." Often perches in overhanging limbs with wings spread wide. Can soar to great heights on flat wings, fanned tail evident but long neck not always apparent.

Strangely proportioned, with long, broad tail and thin neck, small head, and long straight bill. Male (left) has black head and neck. Female and young bird with beige head and neck. Soars easily and often, on broad, slightly pointed wings, tail often fanned.

Double-crested Cormorant

Phalacrocorax auritus

L 33" | **WS** 50"

Lanky and reptilian, the Double-crested Cormorant is a
common to locally abundant, and apparently increasing,
permanent resident in both North and South Carolina. At
home in both salt and freshwater, cormorants congregate in
the hundreds of thousands along the coast, blacking out some
dredge islands with their dense flocks. Large reservoirs and
lakes inland see flocks that number only in the hundreds,
floating low on the water or perched upright on snags with
wings often outspread. Most abundant in winter, when resident
flocks are inflated by migrants from the north.

Sits on snags, pylons, and jetties. Upright posture, often
with wings spread, shortish tail. Oily black plumage, long
neck, slender hooked bill. Orange patch on the chin and
lore. Immature (right) brownish on the neck and head.

Great Cormorant

Phalacrocorax carbo

L 34" | **WS** 51–63"

Uncommon and local in winter in the Carolinas, the robust, block-headed Great Cormorant is typically found perched high atop pilings, jetties, and rocky groins in coastal inlets. Individuals or small loose groups are generally found in the vicinity of Double-crested Cormorants. When these two species are seen near to one another, Great Cormorant is told by it shorter-tail and chunkier shape. Annual in small numbers at Oregon Inlet and Masonboro Inlet in North Carolina. Much rarer in South Carolina, but occasionally found at Huntington Beach State Park. Very rare inland.

Heavy body, rectangular head, and short tail give an overall bulky impression. White chin patch apparent when seen well, and younger birds are whitish on belly.

American White Pelican

Pelecanus erythrorhynchos

L 50-65" | **WS** 96-114"

Formerly a rare winter visitor to the Carolinas, the massive and unmistakable American White Pelican is now fairly common and increasing along the coasts of both states. Prefers shallow freshwater impoundments or tidal basins, where flocks cruise along slowly in formation, dipping their massive bills into the water for small fish. Can be seen in great numbers at Pea Island NWR in North Carolina and Cape Romain NWR in South Carolina, but increasing in the southern part of Pamlico Sound and all along the South Carolina coast. Seems front-heavy in flight, with long wings and lazy wingbeats. Often soars.

Enormous and almost entirely white. Long orange-yellow bill, orange feet. Heavy-bodied and long billed. All white with black flight feathers. White tail. Neck curled back to rest on the body.

Brown Pelican

Pelecanus occidentalis

L 39-54″ **WS** 79″

It's impossible to spend a day near the ocean in either Carolina without seeing squadrons of goofy-looking Brown Pelicans cruising single-file up and down the beach. Unlike the more tolerant White Pelican, Brown Pelicans prefer salt water almost exclusively, where they catch bait fish with spectacular, graceful plunge dives from heights of 20 feet or more. Dapper adults and uniform brown young birds often rest on pilings, piers, or sandbars, usually spaced evenly. Front-heavy, with large bill and short tail, when sitting on open water. Rare on inland lakes and reservoirs.

Adult (left) large-bodied, with thick legs, small head, and enormous pale bill. Breeding plumage includes chocolate-brown stripes on the neck and creamy yellow wash on the head. Young bird (below) uniformly dingy brown. Adult plumage takes a few years to acquire, and "teenage" birds with features of both young and adult are common.

Wood Stork
Mycteria americana

L 33-45" | **WS** 59-69"

Once federally listed as endangered, the large, bare-headed
Wood Stork is a real conservation success story, reflected by its
ever-expanding range in the Carolinas. Present year-round but
more common in the warmer months, Wood Storks can be found
in freshwater and brackish marshes along the coast of South
Carolina to the North Carolina border. Good spots include
Pinckney Island NWR and Huntington Beach State Park in
South Carolina, Twin Lakes in North Carolina. Often seen
soaring among flocks of vultures, they're prone to late summer
wandering to the north and west, turning up in the Piedmont
with increasing regularity.

Extremely large and long-legged, entirely white
body. Head and neck bare in adults, neck
feathered in young birds. Long bill, drooping at the
tip. Often soars with vultures. Long legs and neck
make a distinctive profile. Underside white with
black flight feathers, tail.

American Bittern

Botaurus lentiginosus

L 28″ | **WS** 36–42″

A strange, secretive heron of freshwater and brackish marshes, American Bittern is fairly common in winter and migration but infrequently seen. In the Carolinas, bitterns are mostly associated with extensive cattail marshes, where they creep slowly through the vegetation and characteristically freeze when spotted, often pointing their bill skyward. Most common in the Coastal Plain, on Bodie and Pea Islands, or at Mattamuskeet NWR in North Carolina, and at Huntington Beach State Park or Savannah NWR in South Carolina. Call, often heard when flushed, a croaking *RAWK*.

Medium-sized and strangely proportioned for a heron, with long, thick neck and relatively short legs. Coarse brown-on-white streaking on the front, subtle browns and tans on the back. In flight, shows contrasting dark wings.

Least Bittern

Ixobrychus exilis

L 13" | **WS** 17"

The smallest heron in North America, the dainty Least Bittern is a fairly common but reclusive breeding bird in freshwater and brackish marshes of coastal South Carolina, less common and less regular in North Carolina. Prefers tall cattail marshes or dense cordgrass stands. Least Bitterns clamber through the vegetation, hunting while suspended gracefully between two stalks. Places like Savannah NWR or Magnolia Gardens in South Carolina or Mackay Island NWR and Cedar Island NWR in North Carolina host them from March through September. When flushed, large buffy patches on the upperwings apparent. Call a soft, descending *ku-ku-ku-ku*.

Compact body, with long legs and toes. Streaked neck, but otherwise warm buffy all over. Male has dark back and cap, female generally paler. When flushed, large tan patches on the forewing apparent.

Green Heron
Butorides virescens

L 18" | **WS** 26"

Richly colored and compact, Green Heron is a common, if
secretive, breeding bird across the whole of both Carolinas. It
can be found along the margins of nearly any freshwater pond,
impoundment, or swamp, perched motionless in the overhanging vegetation waiting for an unsuspecting fish or tadpole
to approach. Green Herons can be found mostly from April
through October, but are year-round on the coast, particularly
in southern South Carolina. Often detected when flushed, gives
an explosive *sKOW* as it escapes.

Small, neck long but mostly held tightly coiled.
Often crouches. Adult with rich rufous on the neck
and various greens and grays on body. Bill thick and
black, legs orange. Young birds similar but more
heavily streaked on the neck. Small and stocky in
flight. Looks front-heavy. Wings broad and rounded.
Short legs barely extend beyond tail.

Great Blue Heron

Ardea herodias

L 38-54" | **WS** 66-79"

The large Great Blue Heron is familiar to birders and most non-birders alike. Common across the entirety of both states, Great Blues can be found on nearly any body of fresh or brackish water, and will hunt and eat just about anything they can catch. They can be found year-round, but are most abundant in late summer, when post-breeding birds disperse across the land-scape, often congregating in loose groups on shallow lake arms, impoundments, and marshes. Recalls a pterosaur in flight, with slow, steady wingbeats, neck curled, and long legs dragging behind. Voice, often heard when disturbed, is a cranky *rrRAWK*.

Tall, with long snaking neck, heavy bill. Blue-gray all over, paler on neck, with black and white pattern on head. Long, broad wings, pale in front with dark flight feathers. Slow wingbeats. Long legs dangling behind. Neck coiled.

Great Egret

Ardea alba

L 39″ | **WS** 54″

Lean and elegant, the Great Egret is the most widely distributed
white heron in the Carolinas. It is easily seen in coastal marshes,
where it stalks prey slowly and deliberately along the edges.
Most common on the Coastal Plain, where it can be found at any
time of year, it is also a regular late summer visitor well inland,
where it prefers shallow muddy arms of reservoirs. Breeds in
colonies along the immediate coast with other species of wading
birds. Call is a gravely croak, often given when disturbed.

Large and entirely white, with a very
long neck. Legs black, bill yellow.
Breeding-season adults have a spot of
turquoise between eye and bill, plain
yellow at other times of the year.

Snowy Egret

Egretta thula

L 24" | **WS** 36-39"

A fairly common wading bird of coastal marshes, the lithe and active Snowy Egret is stunning in its breeding finery. Most evident in the warmer months, but some overwinter, particularly towards the south coast of the region. Feeds in a variety of shallow fresh or brackish ponds, marshes, and mudflats, and occasionally even on saltwater inlets and tidal flats. More mobile in its hunting style than other herons, the Snowy Egret often splashes through shallow water, wings askew, in pursuit of small fish. Regular but rare inland in late summer, among assemblages of wading birds on shallow muddy reservoir arms.

Medium-sized, neck long but often coiled. Bill black with yellow lores, legs black with yellow or yellow-orange "slippers." In breeding plumage, covered in fine plumes on neck, head, and back. Young birds similar but lack plumes; legs greenish-yellow on the back.

Little Blue Heron

Egretta caerulea

L 24″ | **WS** 36–40″

The Little Blue Heron is, in many ways, a photo-negative version of Snowy Egret. It's similar in size and shape, but has a stronger preference for freshwater and is more commonly found away from the immediate coast. Little Blues are deliberate hunters, wading slowly through shallow water with neck often extended. A permanent resident in both Carolinas, the species is more common in the warmer months. Little Blue Herons undergo a significant transformation after their first year, turning from an all-white juvenile plumage to the smart gray-blue adult. Birds in the midst of this transition are a motley mix of dark and light. Uncommon inland, mostly in late summer, and like many herons, the young, white birds tend to be more prone to wandering than the adults.

Medium-sized. Adult (above) with slate-blue body, more reddish on neck and head. Bill heavy, bicolored, gray at base with a black tip. Legs greenish gray. Young birds (right) entirely white, becoming piebald as they mature.

Tricolored Heron

Egretta tricolor

L 26″ | **WS** 36″

Thin-necked with a markedly slender bill, the Tricolored Heron has a distinctly coastal distribution in the Carolinas, preferring brackish and salt water more than other medium-sized waders. Fairly common in the warmer months, less so in winter, it breeds in mixed-species colonies on coastal islands. An active feeder, it can be seen chasing bait fish on tidal flats and in salt marshes. In flight, sharply bicolored wings are evident. Breeding-plumage adults striking with bicolored bill and dark legs, changing to yellowish legs and an all-dark bill with a pale lower mandible once nesting is over.

Medium-sized, with long, thin neck. Bill bicolored, bluish base and black tip in breeding plumage, all dark with pale lower mandible the rest of the year. Dark breast, white belly and underwings unique in all plumages. Thin white stripe on front of neck. Young bird (right) with reddish neck, blotchy reddish and blue back. Yellow-green legs and bill. White belly and underwings unique.

Reddish Egret

Egretta rufescens

L 30" | **WS** 46"

Uncommon in the Carolinas, and with an almost exclusive preference for salt water, the disheveled Reddish Egret is madcap in both appearance and behavior. A casual breeder in the southern extreme of the region, it's more commonly a late summer post-breeding visitor to tidal flats along the immediate coast, as far north as southeastern North Carolina. Its frantic foraging style, in which it careers across a tidal basin with wings outstretched, is distinctive even at a distance. Two morphs occur, with dark birds predominating in the Carolinas. Huntington Beach State Park in South Carolina is a fair place to find them. In North Carolina, found near Brunswick County beaches most years.

Medium-sized; dark-morph adult with slate-gray body, maroon neck and head, and sharply bicolored bill with pink base and black tip. Legs black. An active feeder, running about with wings spread. Young birds lanky, with uniformly slate-gray plumage, black bill and legs.

Black-crowned Night-Heron

Nycticorax nycticorax

L 25″ | **WS** 44″

A strange, big-eyed, nocturnal heron, the Black-crowned Night-Heron is most often seen at dawn or dusk as it shuttles to and from the brackish marshes and tidal flats where it forages. During the day it often sits quietly in dense coastal shrubs, where it is infrequently seen despite being a fairly common permanent resident along the coast of both Carolinas. Uncommon inland in migration. Good spots for finding birds during the day include Mattamuskeet and Pea Island NWRs, or Arlie Gardens in North Carolina, Huntington Beach State Park or Pinckney Island NWR in South Carolina. Call a hollow *KWOK*.

Medium-sized. Adult distinctive with pale gray body, black cap, and black back. Thick, sharp bill; yellow legs.

Young bird (below) covered in thick, indistinct streaks, with large teardrop-shaped white spots on back and wings. Thick, sharp bill mostly yellow.

Yellow-crowned Night-Heron

Nyctanassa violacea

L 24″ | **WS** 42″

Slender and inconspicuous, with a striking face pattern, the Yellow-crowned Night-Heron is not quite as nocturnal as its name would suggest, often foraging by day as well as at night. Its distribution in the Carolinas is strange: While fairly common on the coast, it's also known from small nesting colonies in urban centers such as Charleston, Charlotte, Greensboro, and Durham. Mostly a summer resident, it can be found year-round on the south coast of South Carolina. Call is a squawking *keeAWK*.

Medium-sized, with gray body and flashy skunk pattern on the head. Yellow legs. Bill, thick and black, appears blunt. Young birds grayish, with narrow, shorter streaks on front of neck and breast. Tiny white spots on back and wings.

Cattle Egret

Bubulcus ibis

L 20″ | **WS** 36″

The squat, straw-billed Cattle Egret has quite different manners from the rest of its family. Unlike other herons, it's not often found in wetlands, preferring roadsides, sod farms, or pastures. Often seen with livestock, where it feeds on insects and small reptiles kicked up by cattle or horses. Declining across the Carolinas as pastures are re-purposed for agriculture, they are still fairly common across the Coastal Plain in South Carolina as far north as the Cape Fear River in North Carolina. Uncommon elsewhere.

Small and short-legged. Fairly thick neck. Nonbreeding bird entirely white, with stocky yellow bill and black legs. Breeding bird (shown) has yellow legs, buffy orange patches on head, neck, and back.

White Ibis

Eudocimus albus

L 24" | **WS** 39–42"

A smaller wading bird with a perpetually bemused expression, the
White Ibis is a common permanent resident along the coast and
on the Coastal Plain, particularly in South Carolina and southern
North Carolina. Often seen in flocks of a dozen or more foraging
on mudflats or in shallow swamps, and occasionally in salt water
or even on manicured lawns. It uses its long bill to probe the
mud at the edge of the water for aquatic worms and crustaceans.
Generally found among other waders or flying in a shallow V
formation between preferred foraging sites. Uncommon visitor to
muddy reservoirs inland in late summer.

Medium-sized. Adults almost entirely
white, with red face and long,
recurved red bill. Legs red. In flight,
note extended neck, black wingtips.

Young birds mostly brown with
white bellies, turning entirely
white as they age. Bill and legs
more orangey-pink.

Glossy Ibis
Plegadis falcinellus

L 23" | **WS** 36"

With its shiny metallic plumage and subdued demeanor , Glossy Ibis is an easily overlooked permanent resident along the coast of both Carolinas. Preferring shallow freshwater and brackish marshes where it probes for invertebrates with its decurved bill, it's less common than most other waders but can be found somewhat reliably at the large refuges in eastern North Carolina like Alligator River, Mattamuskeet, and Pea Island, and at Bear Island or Savannah NWR in South Carolina. Not generally prone to wander inland like other wading birds, and rare in the Piedmont and west.

Medium-sized. Entirely brown, shiny green on wings and back. Gray bill long, decurved. Breeding adults have blue lines surrounding face, absent on young and non-breeding birds.

Roseate Spoonbill

Platalea ajaja

L 32″ | **WS** 50″

Unmistakable with a rosy-pink body, bald head, and bizarre spatulate bill, Roseate Spoonbill is increasing as a late summer visitor to the South Carolina coast, as far north as Huntington Beach State Park. Fond of marshy impoundments or tidal flats, spoonbills feed by waving their incredible bill back and forth, filtering invertebrates from shallow water. Can be found in sometimes large numbers from June through October at Savannah NWR, Botany Bay, and Bear Island in South Carolina. Less than annual in North Carolina, generally among Wood Storks in the southeast extreme of the state.

Medium-sized. Adults bizarre looking with bright pink body, brightest at the shoulder. Bill long and flattened at the tip. Head bald and occasionally greenish.

Young birds pale, blushed pink. Head feathered, bill long and spatulate. Legs dingy gray and pink.

Black Vulture
Coragyps atratus

L 25″ | **WS** 59″

Short-tailed and blocky-winged, Black Vultures are hard to miss on any reasonably sunny day any time of year anywhere in the Carolinas, but they are most common in the summer and on the Coastal Plain. Gregarious and bold, they are commonly seen near major roadways, seeking out easy meals provided by passing automobiles. When feeding, prefers larger prey items, with squabbling flocks quickly forming around road-killed deer. Flight style is less confident than other raptors, with shorter periods of gliding interspersed with quick, shallow flaps. Mostly silent, but feeding birds hiss at one another.

Glossy black body, thick legs. Large gray head with longish bill, feathered cowl. Tail and wings short. Broad wings with white patches towards the tips.

Turkey Vulture

Cathartes aura

L 25–32″ | **WS** 67″

Seemingly effortless in flight, the Turkey Vulture is the more commonly seen vulture in the Carolinas, and likely the most commonly seen bird of prey, period. Less gregarious than Black Vultures, but still prone to forming loose groups at roost sites on snags or cell phone towers. Turkey Vultures favor smaller prey like raccoons or opossums, which they find with their extraordinary sense of smell. In flight, soars on long rectangular wings held in a shallow V, often teetering back and forth. Rarely flaps once aloft. Mostly silent.

Body more brownish than black, legs pale. Wingtips long, often projecting beyond long tail. Small bare red head with pale bill. Wings and tail very long. Wings black on the forewing, silvery gray on flight feathers, with distinct "fingers." Head very small, inconspicuous.

Golden Eagle

Aquila chrysaetos

L 30″ | **WS** 70–80″

The imposing Golden Eagle is a rare resident in fall and winter, primarily in North Carolina. Its distribution in the state is curious, as it can be found in both the mountains and on the northern Coastal Plain, but generally not in the populated middle of the Piedmont. Most years see a few spending the winter at the large refuges on the Albemarle Peninsula, and some are usually seen in the mountains in the colder months. They are large birds that range widely and are rarely tied to one location for long.

Most individuals in the Carolinas are younger birds. Head fairly small, wings with white patches in the center. Tail white with black tip. Flies with wings held in a slight V, like Turkey Vulture.

Osprey
Pandion haliaetus

L 23″ | **WS** 63″

The piebald, crook-winged Osprey was hit hard by DDT poisoning in the middle of the last century. Since the federal ban on the pesticide went into effect, this "fish hawk" has rebounded in a huge way, helped along by nesting platforms installed on the coast and at several large reservoirs like Jordan Lake, Falls Lake, and Lake Norman in North Carolina and Lake Marion and Lake Murray in South Carolina. Ospreys are common on large bodies of water mostly from March to November, and increasingly in winter. They hunt for fish with spectacular plunge dives. Calls are an incessant piercing *hyep-hyep-hyep-hyep*.

Large, with long wingtips. Entirely dark upperparts and white underneath. Boldly patterned head with dark eye stripe, white crown, large eye. Legs gray.

Appears to be mostly wings in flight, body relatively small. Long wings, slightly pointed, almost always held with a crook at the wrists. Mostly white underneath, dark patches on wrists.

Swallow-tailed Kite

Elanoides forficatus

L 22" | **WS** 48–51"

The elegant, unmistakable Swallow-tailed Kite may be the most spectacular raptor in North America. Fairly common in the lower Santee and Savannah River Basin from April through August, annual but infrequent as far north as southeastern North Carolina. It's most often seen in flight, coursing over swampland in the South Carolina Coastal Plain, snatching small reptiles and large insects out of the treetops and devouring them on the wing. In late summer, will mass for brief periods to gorge on grasshopper swarms. Wanderers can turn up just about anywhere in the Carolinas.

Rarely seen perched. Boldly black and white. Long pointed wings, long forked tail. Eyes large and dark, small black bill.

Mississippi Kite
Ictinia mississippiensis

L 14″ | **WS** 31–35″

Dainty and graceful, the little Mississippi Kite is a fairly common hawk, mostly on the Coastal Plain between April and September. They feed almost exclusively on large flying insects like cicadas and dragonflies, often spiraling hundreds of feet into the air in pursuit. While generally associated with bottom-land forests and agricultural areas in the east, they occasionally nest well into the Piedmont, in well-forested neighborhoods in cities like Charlotte, Greensboro, and Columbia. Highly migratory, they are usually scarce by the end of September, but mass in late summer and fall where insects are swarming.

Fairly small; entirely gray, palest on head and darkest on wingtips. Eye large, surrounded by black.

Wings narrow and pointed. Tail long and, in younger birds, barred. Similar to falcons, but with more graceful flight.

Bald Eagle
Haliaeetus leucocephalus

L 33" | **WS** 80"

The formidable Bald Eagle is familiar to almost every Carolinian. Formerly quite rare across the region, populations of our national bird have increased dramatically in recent years, and now there is scarcely a large body of water in either state where Bald Eagles can't be seen. Primarily eats fish, but keen to take waterfowl when available. They're common at places like Jordan Lake and Lake Norman in the NC Piedmont and Lake Marion and Lake Murray in SC, where they often stake out a tall tree with a commanding view. Not too proud for an easy meal, they congregate in impressive numbers in eastern North Carolina in the vicinity of catfish farms. Call is a series of cackling whistles.

Adults are hard to mistake. Chocolate brown body, white tail and large, blocky white head. Massive yellow bill. Large yellow feet.

n flight, wings are long, broad, and straight, like a plank. Head large and prominent.

Juvenile entirely brown; takes several years to reach adult plumage. In all plumages, note heavy square head and massive bill. Lower legs unfeathered.

Northern Harrier

Circus cyaneus

L 18″ | **WS** 43″

A bird of open country, marshes, and pastures, the lithe and graceful Northern Harrier is a fairly common resident from September through April, particularly along the coast and on the Coastal Plain. The harrier courses low over the landscape, teetering on long wings seeking rodents and small birds. Its owl-like facial disc aids in hearing prey (rodents and small birds) in thick cover. Wildlife refuges with extensive marshes, like Cedar Island NWR in North Carolina and Santee Coastal Reserve in South Carolina, host decent numbers. Mostly silent in the Carolinas.

Adult male unlike any other raptor, pale gray with black wingtips, conspicuous white rump. Skinny body. Very long legs, long narrow tail, long narrow wings in all plumages.

Females variably brown and streaked with buff, barred flight feathers.

Young birds fairly dark-breasted, with unmarked buffy belly. Often perches on the ground in open areas.

Sharp-shinned Hawk

Accipiter striatus

L 11″ | **WS** 21″

The smaller of our two regular accipiters — bird-hunting hawks with short wings and long tails — the Sharp-shinned Hawk is a fairly common migrant and uncommon winter resident in the Carolinas. Fall migrants are generally seen after the first cold front, peaking in mid-October, primarily along the coast and at hawkwatch sites in the mountains, such as Caesar's Head in western South Carolina. Secretive when perched. Wingbeats snappy with frequent short glides, wrists pushed forward on outstretched wing, and head small, giving the impression of a "flying gavel."

Small and top-heavy. Broader at the chest than at the waist. Adult with gray back, red-barred breast. Head rounded, bill quite small. Hooded, with crown and nape same color. Eyes prominent, giving a permanently surprised expression. Tail long, generally square-tipped. Immature birds with brown back, fine streaking on breast. In flight, all ages show short rounded wings pushed forward at the wrists, small head. Long square-tipped tail.

Cooper's Hawk
Accipiter cooperii

L 16″ | **WS** 28″

Fierce and fast, Cooper's Hawk is a common and increasing permanent resident across the Carolinas. Fairly catholic in its habitat choices, they are seen as often in suburban and urban environments as they are in forests and brushy fields, often taking advantage of congregations of birds in cities, especially at feeding stations. Most common in fall and winter, when birds from farther north augment the population. Like Sharp-shinned, often seen in flight. Wingbeats choppy with frequent glides. Wings held straight across on the leading edge, with large head conspicuous, like a "flying cross." Vocal, particularly when nesting; call a nasal *ack-ack-ack-ack*.

Tall and thin, shaped like a bowling pin. Equally broad at chest and waist. Adults with gray back, red-barred breast. Head flat-topped, heavy brow, bill fairly large, giving a fierce expression. Black cap and pale nape distinctive. Tail long and generally rounded at the tip. Immatures with brown back, sparse teardrop streaks on breast. In flight, wings long and straight across at the leading edge. Head large and prominent. Tail long and mostly rounded at tip.

Red-shouldered Hawk

Buteo lineatus

L 20″ | **WS** 40″

Fond of wooded suburban areas, the classy Red-shouldered Hawk is probably the raptor birders are most likely to see near their homes, particularly in the Piedmont. A common year-round resident across the Carolinas, they are generally found near swamps, impoundments, and retention ponds, where they can find their preferred prey of frogs and snakes. Red-shouldered Hawks are particularly noisy in late winter and spring when courting, and again in summer when young leave the nest. The calls are emphatic, clear, down-slurred whistles.

Adult reddish on breast. Black and white barring on wings and narrow white bands on black tail.

Fairly long wings, long tail. All plumages show pale "crescent" across the outer flight feathers of the wing.

Broad-winged Hawk

Buteo platypterus

L 15″ | **WS** 34″

Highly migratory with short, pointed wings, the Broad-winged Hawk is a locally abundant migrant and uncommon breeding bird in the Carolinas, particularly in the western third. Mostly retiring in the breeding season, Broad-wings prefer unbroken forests, behavior and habitat that puts them out of the way of most birders in the state. Most birds are seen in fall when "kettles," large spiraling tornados of migrating birds, form over Appalachian ridges, drifting high into the sky as they move south. Hawkwatch sites such as Grandfather Mountain and Pilot Mountain in North Carolina and, especially, Caesar's Head in South Carolina see hundreds or thousands pass by on a good day in September or October. Can be vocal; call a high, piercing whistle.

Adult (left) compact with pale underwings with distinct black margin. Smudgy reddish-brown markings mostly limited to upper breast. White chin. Immature bird (below) with pale underwing and indistinctly marked tail. Broad streaking on underside, densest on breast.

Red-tailed Hawk

Buteo jamaicensis

L 19" | **WS** 49"

Broad-bodied and broad-winged, the Red-tailed Hawk is one of our most well-known raptors, a familiar permanent resident of open country across both Carolinas. Red-tails hunt primarily mammals from a prominent location, often perching near roadways on snags and utility poles with a commanding view of surrounding fields and pastures. Soars effortlessly with tail spread wide. Familiar call a hoarse scream, *KEEEyer!*

Broad-chested and large-headed. Adult with dark hood, dark brown bac and pale front. White V on shoulders and back. Dark belly band. Brick red tail.

Long, broad wings, prominent head, broad shortish tail. Belly band is conspicuous from beneath.

Immature birds more finely marked, narrow bands on brownish tail. Underparts cleaner white, with more prominent belly band

Clapper Rail
Rallus crepitans

L 14″ | **WS** 19″

The chicken-sized Clapper Rail is the easiest of a generally secretive family of birds (Rallidae) to see in the Carolinas. Typically a common permanent resident of cordgrass salt marshes along the coast, Clapper Rails can sometimes be seen at expansive brackish sites a bit inland, where confusion with the similar King Rail is common. They creep between grasses probing for crustaceans and worms, occasionally coming out onto exposed flats at low tide. Good places to find Clapper Rails include Bodie Lighthouse, Cedar Island NWR, and Fort Fisher in North Carolina, and Huntington Beach State Park, Pinckney NWR, and even Charleston Harbor in South Carolina. More often heard than seen; call a grunting series *kik-kik-kik*.

Chicken-sized, long greenish legs and dull yellow bill. Dingy gray and indistinctly marked all over, with faint black and white barring on the flanks.

King Rail
Rallus elegans

L 17" | **WS** 20"

The freshwater counterpart of the drab Clapper Rail, the richly colored King Rail is an uncommon and reclusive denizen of cattail marshes, mostly on the Coastal Plain. Overlaps with Clapper Rail in some brackish marshes along the coast, and some individuals with intermediate features may be hybrids or simply unidentifiable. Most reliable at Mackay Island NWR or the USS North Carolina Memorial in North Carolina, or at Savannah NWR or Magnolia Gardens in South Carolina. Calls similar to Clapper Rail, but slower and deeper, *kek, kek, kek*.

Chicken-sized, long gray legs and yellowish bill. Head gray, contrasting with rich orange neck and breast. Black and white barring on flanks fairly bold. Bold streaks on back.

Virginia Rail

Rallus limicola

L 9″ | **WS** 13″

Furtive and mysterious, the Virginia Rail is a reasonably
common winter resident across the eastern half of both
Carolinas and a breeding bird in scattered brackish marshes
near the coast. It can occasionally be seen walking along the
muddy edges of marshes at low tide, but prefers to spend time
in dense cover, where it can be hard to see unless inadvertently
flushed. Calls mostly at dawn and dusk; can usually be heard,
if not seen, at places like Bodie Lighthouse, Fort Fisher, and
Cedar Island NWR in North Carolina, and Savannah NWR and
Huntington Beach State Park in South Carolina. Calls include
a metallic *hink-hiddinnk-hiddinnk* and a descending series of
wheezy grunts.

Like a small King Rail. Compact, with
shorter legs, long reddish bill. Dark
gray face contrasts with rufous neck
and sides. Fine black and white barring
on flanks. Very dark in flight.

Sora
Porzana carolina

L 9″ | **WS** 14″

The stout, short-billed Sora is a common migrant and winter resident in the Carolinas. Preferring freshwater marshes along the coast, they can turn up just about anywhere in migration, and often put down in wet meadows or ephemeral sedge stands in the Piedmont and even the mountains. Often walks in the open at the edge of marshes, constantly flicking its short white tail. Good spots include Mattamuskeet NWR and the USS North Carolina Memorial in North Carolina, Savannah NWR and Magnolia Gardens in South Carolina. Common call is a long, shrill, descending whinny, which can be prompted from the bird fairly readily by clapping hands, whistled imitations, or even slamming a car door nearby.

Stocky, with bright yellow legs and short yellow bill. Black mask, gray head and breast. White undertail. Finely marked back and sides.

Purple Gallinule

Porphyrio martinicus

L 13″ | **WS** 22″

Unabashedly tropical-looking in purples, greens, and blues, the Purple Gallinule is a large, unmistakable rail. It reaches the northern extent of its range in South Carolina, where it is a common breeding bird in the lower Savannah River drainage, primarily at Savannah NWR and Donnelly Wildlife Management Area. Preferring calm freshwater ponds with lots of water lilies, it strides across the vegetation, its weight distributed by long, yellow toes. Uncommon to rare as far north as southern North Carolina, Purple Gallinules are prone to wandering and can show up just about anywhere. Calls include a variety of thin honks.

Adults with impossible purple and turquoise body. Long yellow legs. Red bill, pale blue shield or forehead. White undertail. Immature birds pale brown with greenish wings, dark bill.

Common Gallinule

Gallinula galeata

L 14″ | **WS** 21″

A year-round resident of quiet, vegetated ponds along the coast, Common Gallinule is hard to miss in South Carolina, though more infrequent to the north. Unlike most rails, it is primarily a swimmer, cruising from one hiding spot to the next, bobbing its neck like a waterborne pigeon. Very common from the Savannah River to Charleston, can be easily seen on ponds and impoundments in the entire region. Regular in North Carolina at Mattamuskeet NWR or Arlie Gardens near Wilmington. Call a raucous series of bubbly clucks, like laughter.

Adult mostly black with distinctive white slash along the side. Bill red with yellow tip, red shield on forehead. White around tail. Immature birds uniformly gray, with darker wings, gray bill. Most show some white slash on the side.

American Coot

Fulica americana

L 15" | **WS** 24"

Dense, churning flocks of American Coots are a common winter sight on most bodies of fresh or brackish water in the Carolinas. Versatile feeders, coots dive for food in shallow water, pick items from the surface, or wander on the shore, padding about on bizarre-looking lobed feet. Present mostly from October through April, some stick around through the summer, occasionally breeding in freshwater marshes on the Coastal Plain. Flocks are very vocal, making a variety of chirpy peeps, honks, and clucks.

Almost entirely black. Rounded head and body, small white bill with black band, reddish forehead shield.

Sandhill Crane

Grus canadensis

L 47" | **WS** 78"

Easily the tallest bird in the Carolinas, the impressive Sandhill Crane is an uncommon migrant and an unpredictable winter visitor across both states. Most cranes in the Carolinas are from a population the breeds in the eastern Great Lakes region and winters in Florida, passing through the region between November and March. Despite their resemblance to herons, cranes are not usually seen in wetlands, preferring wide-open places like plowed fields and pastures, typically on the Coastal Plain. Call is a loud, rolling bugle.

Very tall, with long legs and neck. Large gray body, shaggy feathers near tail. Red crown, long black bill.

In flight, long neck extended, not coiled. Wings long and broad, legs extend well beyond short tail.

Black-necked Stilt

Himantopus mexicanus

L 14″ | **WS** 29″

Striking in black and white with impossibly long legs, the Black-necked Stilt is hard to miss. It's a common summer resident in freshwater and brackish marshes near the coast, generally more common in the south than in the north. Quite rare elsewhere. Graceful and deliberate feeders, stilts pick at food on the surface of the water with their needle-like bills, often alone or in small, loose flocks. Common in South Carolina, particularly at Bear Island or Savannah Spoil Area, regular in North Carolina at Pea Island NWR. Call a harsh *pik-pik-pik*, often given in flight.

Boldly patterned, with black back, neck, and crown. White belly, breast, and front of neck. Incredibly long reddish legs. Needle-like black bill.

American Avocet

Recurvirostra americana

L 18″ | **WS** 31″

The distribution of the elegant, bow-billed American Avocet
in the Carolinas is exceedingly strange and hyper-local. It is
very rare in either state except in marshes at Pea Island NWR
in North Carolina and Bear Island and Savannah Spoil Area
in South Carolina, where flocks of up to 200 have overwin-
tered for years, with a few lingering year-round. Exquisite and
distinctive in black and white, avocets feed by swishing their
curved bill back and forth through shallow to belly-deep water,
often many birds in unison. Roosts in a tight flock, standing in
shallow water with head tucked into back. Call is a high *keep!*

Very tall and long-legged. Thin bill, strongly
upturned. Wings black with white stripe at
the shoulder. Head and neck pale gray.
Breeding birds (late spring and summer)
have apricot head and neck.

Black-bellied Plover

Pluvialis squatarola

L 11″ | **WS** 23″

Round with a stout baton-like bill, Black-bellied Plover is a common wintering shorebird on the coast and a rare to uncommon, mostly fall, migrant inland. Birders in the Carolinas rarely get to see the dapper black-bellied breeding plumage for which the bird is named, as most occur in the region in plain gray non-breeding garb. Alert and nervous, they can be found on any tidal flats or beaches in season, running quickly across the sand and stopping abruptly. Call a keening whistle, *pyoEEEE*.

Large for a plover, with rounded head and thick bill. Nonbreeding birds mostly mottled gray, paler on breast and belly. In flight, black "wingpits" are distinctive.

Birds begin molting into breeding plumage before they leave in spring. Checkerboard back, messy and variable black mottling on face, breast, and flanks.

American Golden-Plover
Pluvialis dominica

L 10″ | **WS** 22″

Delicate, with long wings, American Golden-Plover is an uncommon but annual fall migrant in the Carolinas. While it can occasionally be found on sand flats or inland mudflats, they are most commonly seen in areas where grass is cropped close, like sod farms, sports fields, or airports. Good spots include turf farms in Washington County, North Carolina, and Orangeburg, South Carolina, in September and October. Call is a plaintive *tooWHEET*.

Non-breeding birds pale brownish all over, palest on belly. Round head with slender black bill, large eye and dark cap. Wings extremely long, extending well beyond tip of the tail.

Wilson's Plover

Charadrius wilsonia

L 8″ | **WS** 16″

The largest of the single-banded plovers in the Carolinas, Wilson's Plover is an uncommon and generally local breeding bird, found along the immediate coast from March through October. They nest on sand flats, and are thus sensitive to human and vehicle traffic on beaches, and forage mostly at inlets and on tidal flats away from human disturbance. The largest concentrations are on the most inaccessible barrier islands. Compared to other plovers, they are long-legged and very large-billed. Rather rare north of Carteret County, good places to find them include the north end of Wrightsville Beach in North Carolina and Huntington Beach State Park or Savannah Spoil Site in South Carolina. Call a bubbly *kiddit*.

Large-headed, with a massive bill. Gray-brown on back, white underneath. Breeding birds with single thick, breast band, small black cap on head. White forehead. Pinkish-gray legs. In flight, white band on wing, tail with black tip and white outer feathers.

Non-breeding and immature birds in late summer paler gray, breast band thinner and gray. Large black bill obvious.

Semipalmated Plover

Charadrius semipalmatus

L 7″ | **WS** 14″

The bull-necked little Semipalmated Plover is a common migrant throughout the Carolinas and an uncommon winter resident on the coast. Its dark back offers camouflage on mud and wet sand, and so this species is seen more often on tidal flats, mudflats, and the edges of lakes and ponds than other, more coastally distributed plovers. Most common in August and September on dry arms of reservoirs, often in significant numbers. Typical call is an emphatic *cho-WEEP.*

Small-headed and round. Tiny bicolored bill, orange base with black tip. Orange legs. Breeding birds with dark brown back, white belly, thick black breast band. Black mask and crown. Small white forehead. In flight, shows white bar on wings, black-tipped tail.

Non-breeding birds dark brown on back, breast band more diffuse. Face plain with white chin, forehead, thin white eyebrow.

Piping Plover

Charadrius melodus

L 7″ | **WS** 15″

Few birds in the Carolinas engender as much passion as the cute little Piping Plover. The endangered shorebird has been the flashpoint in a long-running argument about beach access at Cape Hatteras National Seashore, where sections are annually closed to vehicles to protect nesting plovers. They remain an uncommon year-round resident in the Carolinas, breeding at only a few sites in North Carolina, but disperse widely to winter on beaches across the region. Ghostly gray, they blend in perfectly with dry sand above the wrack line where they forage. Reliable in winter at Wrightsville Beach, North Carolina, and Huntington Beach State Park, South Carolina. Call a breezy *PEE-yop*.

Small, round, short-winged. Very small bill. Breeding bird (top left) pale gray on back and face, white belly. Bright orange legs. Bicolored bill, orange-based with black tip. Thin black band around neck, usually broken at breast. Black-bordered white forehead. Non-breeding bird (bottom left) entirely pale gray, yellowish legs. Bill mostly black, some orange at the base of the lower mandible.

Killdeer

Charadrius vociferus

L 10" | **WS** 19"

Easily the most familiar shorebird in the Carolinas, and one
very unlikely to be seen at the shore, the Killdeer is common
year-round on pastures, plowed farmland, sports fields, and
basically any open, short-grass, or shallow freshwater habitat.
Large and noisy, Killdeer are known for their predilection for
laying eggs on gravel roads and parking lots; their elaborate
"broken wing" display is an attempt to draw threats away from
eggs or chicks by feigning injury, only to break away and fly off
once at a safe distance. More common in winter, when numbers
are enhanced by northern migrants. Calls are a seemingly
endless series of loud, piercing *kee-YEEER kee-YEEER* notes,
hence the name, and sputtering *pip-pip-pip-pip*.

Comma-shaped body with long wings and tail. Dark brown on
back, white underneath. Double bands, one around neck and
one across breast. Thin black bill, greenish legs. Black stripe
across cheek, white forehead, white crescent behind eye.

American Oystercatcher

Haematopus palliatus

L 17″ | **WS** 35″

Stocky and strident, the American Oystercatcher is a dramatic, fairly common year-round resident of the immediate coast. While oystercatchers typically nest on sand flats, they forage on tidal flats on the back side of barrier islands or on hard structures such as piers, groins, and jetties, where they are more likely to find the mollusks they feed on. Oystercatchers are vociferous; calls are insistent whistled peeps, singly or strung together in a long series.

Very large. Heavy-set, with thick pink, legs and stocky neck. Black head and neck, dark brown back, white breast and belly. Long, bright red bill. Immature birds similar, but with duller bill.

Spotted Sandpiper
Actitis macularius

L 8″ | **WS** 15″

Few shorebirds are as distinctive as the bouncing Spotted Sandpiper, a common migrant across the Carolinas and uncommon
winter resident on the south coast. Spotteds typically prefer
freshwater, and unlike most other sandpipers, can manage on
even relatively small bodies of water, including river sandbars or
small ponds. They move quickly with head low, chasing insects
and constantly bobbing their back end. Flight distinctive, rapid
stuttery wingbeats interspersed with glides. Migration ends
late in spring and starts early in fall, with birds not gone until
the end of May and arriving again in early July. Flight call, most
often heard when flushed, is a rising *tWEE tWEE tWEE*.

Plump and long-bodied. Breeding
adult heavily spotted below. Relatively
short legs, gray-brown upperparts.
Legs and bill pale orange.

White below, brown on back
extending around the sides of the
breast. Unobtrusive white eye
line. Legs yellow, bill dull.

Ruddy Turnstone

Arenaria interpres

L 7" | **WS** 21"

The colorful little Ruddy Turnstone is unique among shorebirds
for both its harlequin plumage and its remarkable behavior.
Low-slung and short-legged, it creeps methodically along rocky
shorelines or tidal flats, poking at pebbles, shells, and beach
wrack, flipping items over with its unusual, slightly upturned
bill to see what is hiding beneath. Can be found on beaches,
but prefers hard structures like piers and groins, where it often
scurries confidently among fishermen, looking for bait scraps.
Present year-round in the Carolinas, but most common in the
winter. Scarce on inland mudflats, typically in fall. Call, often
given when flushed, a musical chatter.

Bold pattern of breeding
bird distinctive. Reddish
back, unique black and
white pattern on breast
and face. Legs orange,
bill black.

Medium-sized, short legs
and long body. Short bill,
slightly turned up.
Nonbreeding birds messy
brown on back and head,
dark patches on breast.
Legs orange.

Solitary Sandpiper
Tringa solitaria

L 9″ | **WS** 16″

The delicate and aptly named Solitary Sandpiper is generally seen solo or in small loose groups. A widespread migrant
across the Carolinas in both spring and fall, can be found on
the muddy margins of small ponds, grassy puddles, or flooded
fields. In fall, they are often seen on mudflats with other
migrating shorebirds. Present in April and May and again from
July to October, their time in the Carolinas is briefer in spring
than in fall. Call a rapid, thin *weet weet weet*.

Medium-sized, body long and slender.
Prominent eye ring. Round head with
thin, straight bill. Breeding birds
speckled white on the back and neck,
non-breeding birds more subdued. All
with darker breast, greenish legs.

Greater Yellowlegs

Tringa melanoleuca

L 12″ | **WS** 24–28″

A large and conspicuous "marshpiper" with a heavy, slightly upturned bill, the Greater Yellowlegs is a fairly common migrant throughout the Carolinas in both spring and fall and an uncommon wintering bird near the coast. Can be found in both salt and freshwater, in deeper marshes, on mudflats, and on tidal flats. Forages purposefully, striding forward on long yellow legs and often chasing prey through the water. Call is a high-pitched, strident *PEW!*, usually given in a rapid series of three or four.

Fairly large, with very long neck and bright yellow legs. Bill dark, heavy at base, slightly upturned, and longer than the head. Speckled on back and finely streaked on head and neck. Usually shows some barring on the flanks.

Lesser Yellowlegs
Tringa flavipes

L 10″ | **WS** 24″

The graceful Lesser Yellowlegs is similar in most respects
to Greater Yellowlegs. It's a fairly common migrant in both
spring and fall and an uncommon and local winter resident
towards the coast. Generally prefers freshwater, stopping over
on impoundments, grassy ponds, and ephemeral wetlands. An
active feeder, Lesser Yellowlegs plucks food from the surface of
the water with its long, thin bill. Call is a high *cheew-cheew*,
often given in pairs.

Similar to Greater Yellowlegs but
daintier. Long, bright yellow legs.
Very thin black bill not much
longer than head. Speckled on
back, generally pale underneath.

Willet

Tringa semipalmata

L 15″ | **WS** 26″

Heavy-bodied and long-legged, with a striking pied wing pattern in flight, the Willet is among the largest types of shorebird one is likely to see on a beach. Willets can be found year-round, but the wintering and summering populations in the Carolinas are different: Those that breed in sound-side salt marshes in the summer, "Eastern" Willets, migrate to the Caribbean and South America in winter, and are replaced on beaches in the Southeast by paler, longer-billed birds from the west, "Western" Willets. The two populations overlap briefly in spring and fall. Found on beaches or around inlets throughout, but very rare inland. Call is a trumpeting *PER PER-eet*.

Large, with long gray legs and thick bill. "Eastern" birds heavily marked in breeding season, with dense streaking on head and neck.

Overwintering Willets are "Western," overall pale gray, long gray legs. Generally more slender, with slightly upturned bill longer than in breeding birds.

Bold black and white wing pattern on broad wings. "Western" Willet with pale gray tail, "Eastern" Willet darker tail.

Whimbrel

Numenius phaeopus

L 17" | **WS** 32"

A large shorebird with a long down-turned bill, the unique
Whimbrel is a common coastal migrant in the spring and fall.
It prefers extensive tidal flats anywhere along the coastal
barrier islands, but can also be found at inlets or oceanfront
beaches, where they probe for buried invertebrates in wet sand.
Generally present in the Carolinas from April to June and July
to August, sometimes in groups up to 50 in the fall. A Eurasian
subspecies, with a white wedge on the back, has been recorded
in the Carolinas a handful of times. Call a rapid, bubbly
weekweekweekweekweekweek.

Fairly large, heavy-bodied, with
stocky gray legs and a long
curved bill. Back buff and brown,
breast streaked, belly beige. Small
head with bold striped pattern.

Marbled Godwit
Limosa fedoa

L 18″ | **WS** 30″

The largest commonly occurring sandpiper in the Carolinas, the Marbled Godwit nests on the northern Great Plains and winters on extensive mudflats up and down the coast. Marbled Godwits are long-legged, with an extremely long bill used to seek out worms, crustaceans, and mollusks buried in sand and mud. Typically present in the Carolinas from August through April, they can be found fairly easily at the Fort Fisher Basin in North Carolina, or on any of the barrier island beaches between Charleston and the Savannah River in South Carolina. Call a hoarse, barking *KWEYK*, often in a slow string.

Very large, tall, with extremely long, bicolored bill. Mostly buffy, with fine black markings on back. Bill with pink base, black tip. Long legs black.

Red Knot

Calidris canutus

L 10″ | **WS** 23″

The pot-bellied, stout-billed Red Knot is an uncommon and declining migrant in the Carolinas. Populations of this species have crashed in recent years, thought to be the result of over-harvesting of horseshoe crabs in the Chesapeake and Delaware Bays. The species can still be found with some regularity on beaches and tidal flats in migration and winter, typically in flocks of a dozen or less, but masses of several hundred can still be expected every April and May at known stopover sites like Kiawah Island and Folly Beach near Charleston, South Carolina. Flocks make chattery calls and plaintive whistles.

Medium-sized and stocky, with smallish head, baton-like bill. Nonbreeding birds mostly pale gray with white eye stripe. Legs black. Young birds with neatly scalloped feathers on the back.

Breeding birds brick-red on breast and face. Legs gray-green.

Stilt Sandpiper

Calidris himantopus

L 8″ | **WS** 18″

Lanky, with exaggerated features, Stilt Sandpiper is a common migrant in the Carolinas, particularly in fall. Structurally, it is similar to yellowlegs and dowitchers, and often feeds in deeper water among those species. Foraging style is diagnostic even at a distance. Stilt Sandpipers tip their whole body forward, often completely submerging their heads in water, with tail stuck high in the air. Prefers shallow fresh or brackish water, impoundments or muddy ponds, most common near the coast but regular on muddy arms of inland reservoirs. Present in April and May and again from July to October.

Slender and tall, with relatively large head and long, drooping bill. Dull yellow legs. Breeding adult (top) with barred sides and streaked neck. Dark cap, eye line, and neat chestnut patch on the ear. Non-breeding bird (right) mostly grayish. Dull green legs and long, drooping black bill.

Sanderling

Calidris alba

L 8" | **WS** 15"

Scurrying along the shore ahead of the waves like little wind-up toys, Sanderlings are well known to beach-goers. Compact for shorebirds, they're present year-round in the Carolinas, reaching their greatest abundance in fall and spring and least common at the height of summer. They prefer beaches right at the surf, where their pale gray plumage allows them to disappear against the sand. Infrequent inland on muddy arms of reservoirs, typically in fall. Calls are bubbly chirps, given frequently when flushed.

Small, stocky, bull-necked, with a thick black bill. Nonbreeding bird very pale. Legs black.

Breeding adults with rich rufous breast, head, back.

Young birds with neat checkerboard pattern on the back, mostly white face. Seen mostly in late summer into fall.

Dunlin

Calidris alpina

L 8″ | **WS** 15″

Dumpy, with an exceptionally long bill, the Dunlin is a common migrant and winter resident along the coast of both Carolinas. It can be found in all manner of wetland habitats, fresh and salt, from beachfront to the muddy margins of ponds and reservoirs, though it prefers tidal flats and inlets, where thousands may congregate in the late winter. Migration in spring and fall is later than other shorebirds, with arrival generally in late October and departure in late May or early June. Call, occasionally given while foraging, is a burry *cheev*.

Small, stocky, with a very long drooping, bill. Nonbreeding birds mostly gray-brown on back, head, and breast. White underneath. Legs black.

Breeding birds with black belly, pale face, and reddish back and wings. Birds molting in late spring often patchy.

Buff-breasted Sandpiper

Calidris subruficollis

L 8″ | **WS** 18″

Always a great find in the Carolinas, the elegant, doe-eyed Buff-breasted Sandpiper is an uncommon and local fall visitor to sod farms, sports fields, and overgrown mudflats. Fairly reliable for a few weeks in late August and early September at sod farms in Washington County, North Carolina, and Orangeburg County, South Carolina. Uncommon to rare elsewhere in habitats with close-cropped grass, usually among American Golden-Plovers and Pectoral Sandpipers.

Medium-sized and plump. Round head with large eye, slender black bill. Long greenish-yellow legs. Most birds in the Carolinas are young, with finely scalloped pattern on the back.

Purple Sandpiper

Calidris maritima

L 9″ | **WS** 17″

This unique little "rockpiper" reaches the southern extent of its winter range in the Carolinas, and while only a few are present at any time, they show remarkable fidelity to their preferred sites. Purple Sandpipers are found on wave-splashed rocks, in the Carolinas including man-made structures like groins, breakwaters, and piers. There are only a few appropriate sites in the region, but they are fairly reliable at the south side of Oregon Inlet and the south end of Wrightsville Beach in North Carolina and on the pier at Huntington Beach State Park in South Carolina.

Small, short-legged and very dark. Purplish-gray breast, head, and back. Bright orange legs. Drooping bill orange at base.

Pectoral Sandpiper

Calidris melanotos

L 9″ | **WS** 18″

Deep-bellied with a relatively small head, Pectoral Sandpiper is very much like a larger version of the tiny Least Sandpiper. It's a common migrant in spring and, particularly, fall throughout the Carolinas, preferring freshwater mudflats, wet meadows, and sod farms. Much larger than most of the other sandpipers with which it congregates. Prefers to keep its feet dry, foraging on mud above the water line. August and September are generally the best times of year to find large numbers, when migrating birds congregate at sod farms in Washington County, North Carolina, and Orangeburg County, South Carolina, or along the Fort Fisher spit and Savannah Spoil Site. Vocal when flushed; call a rolling *chrrrt chrrrt*.

Medium-sized, portly, and small-headed. Neatly streaked breast abruptly set off from white belly. Legs yellow to yellow-green. Bill slender, narrow at tip.

Least Sandpiper

Calidris minutilla

L 6″ | **WS** 11″

Of the five small sandpipers in the genus *Calidris*, often called "peeps," the Least Sandpiper is both the smallest and the most common in the Carolinas. It's a regular migrant and increasing winter resident across the eastern two-thirds of both states, preferring muddy edges of ponds and reservoirs, open marshes, and occasionally groins and jetties on the coast. A very early fall migrant, often back in the Carolinas as early as July. It prefers to feed on the edge of the water in a distinctive low crouch, belly nearly scraping the mud as it creeps along, appearing almost rodent-like at a distance. Often calls as it flushes in small, tight flocks, a high, quavering *preeeep*.

Very small, alert and nervous. Bill slender and slightly curved, very narrow at the tip. Legs yellow, often crouches low. Breeding birds with broad streaking.

Nonbreeding birds fairly dark brown, with white belly. Legs more green.

White-rumped Sandpiper

Calidris fuscicollis

L 8″ | **WS** 17″

Among the largest of the regularly occurring *Calidris*
sandpipers, the White-rumped Sandpiper is an uncommon
migrant through the Carolinas, passing northward in May and
again southbound from August to October. Fond of freshwater
mudflats near the coast, it is most reliable at Pea Island NWR
in North Carolina or Savannah Spoil Site in South Carolina.
The white rump is seen most often in flight. More notable
are its exceptionally long wings, which extend past the tip of
the tail to give the bird a long, very pointy look, particularly
compared to other shorebirds.

Very long-bodied. Slender
bill and long wingtips look
"pointy." Fine narrow, streaks
on breast. Black legs.

Baird's Sandpiper

Calidris bairdii

L 7.5″ | **WS** 15″

A fairly large "grasspiper," Baird's Sandpiper is an uncommon fall migrant in the Carolinas. Unlike most of its mud-loving kin, it prefers the dry, grassy parts of mudflats, and typically stops over in the Piedmont only in drier years. Most years find them nearer the coast, at sod farms and tidal pools with grassy margins, in late August and early September. Full breast and very long wings.

Most birds in the Carolinas are young, with a buffy wash across the breast and a distinctly scalloped pattern on the back. Relatively long legs and very long wings, often crossed beyond the tail.

Semipalmated Sandpiper

Calidris pusilla

L 6″ | **WS** 11″

The Semipalmated Sandpiper is a common to abundant migrant along the coast, with smaller numbers on reservoirs inland. They are particularly common in fall along the Outer Banks of North Carolina, which is a staging point for birds taking the offshore route to wintering sites in coastal South America. Prefers tidal flats and inlets, where they can be found in great numbers in May and again from August through October. Semipalmated Sandpipers are active feeders, often wading in shallow water, picking at items near their feet. Flocks are vocal, with various chittery churfs and trills.

Small, short-winged, with largish head. Bill short and blunt, mostly same thickness throughout. Splotchy brown-gray above, with dark cap. Fine streaking on breast. Black legs set in the middle of the body. Young birds have neat scaling on the back.

Western Sandpiper

Calidris mauri

L 6" | **WS** 12"

Despite its name, the Western Sandpiper is a common wintering bird on the southeastern coast, and at times is the most abundant bird on Carolina beaches. Similar to Semipalmated Sandpiper, but with a longer, tapered, drooping bill, the two can often be found together in mixed shorebird flocks in spring and fall on tidal flats, inlets, and freshwater mudflats near the coast. Appears slender and front-heavy, and tends to stretch for food well in front of its feet, generally in deeper water. A good find inland, at muddy reservoir arms primarily in fall. Calls are scratchy chirps.

Small and slender. Longer, slightly drooping bill, thinner at tip than base. Smudgy dark gray on back and wings, paler head. Black legs set behind center of body, giving front-heavy appearance.

Young birds in fall fine marked on back, with rufous streak on the shoulder, pale head.

Short-billed Dowitcher

Limnodromus griseus

L 11″ | **WS** 19″

One half of one of the more difficult identification issues Carolina birders are likely to encounter, the Short-billed Dowitcher is the more common of our two dowitcher species, and the only one regularly found in saltwater environments. Stocky and small-headed, with a very long bill, dowitchers forage with distinctive rapid sewing-machine motions as they wade through shallow mud. Most common on the coast and Coastal Plain, this species overwinters in good numbers at Fort Fisher in North Carolina and Donnelly WMA and Huntington Beach State Park in South Carolina. Found on muddy reservoir arms inland mostly in late summer and early fall. Best told from Long-billed Dowitcher by voice, a fluty *chu-chu-chu* given primarily in flight.

Plump, with a small head and very long, straight bill. Nonbreeding birds mostly gray with white eyebrow. Dark barring on flanks. Greenish legs.

Breeding birds with orange blush on breast and face. Richly marked back and sides. Dark cap.

Long-billed Dowitcher

Limnodromus scolopaceus

L 11″ | **WS** 19″

Less common than the Short-billed Dowitcher, and almost exclusively associated with freshwater habitats, Long-billed Dowitcher is an uncommon to rare migrant and winter resident in the Carolinas. Like Short-billeds, they forage in the telltale frantic sewing-machine manner, often among other species of shorebirds. They average longer-faced and more hunchbacked than Short-billed, though the difference is often subtle. Not common anywhere, but fairly reliable at Pea Island and Mattamuskeet NWRs in North Carolina, and at Savannah Spoil Site in South Carolina. Voice is the best way to differentiate: Long-billed Dowitcher gives a sharp *queeck!*, single or paired.

Plump, small-headed, with long straight bill. Very similar to Short-billed Dowitcher, but darker gray, with a longer face. Smudgy o the flanks instead of barred.

Wilson's Snipe

Gallinago delicata

L 10" | **WS** 18"

Secretive and well camouflaged, the Wilson's Snipe is a bird of muddy ditches, wet pastures, and well-vegetated pond shores. Common throughout the Carolinas from September to April, snipe can easily be missed as they hunker down in dense damp cover, rarely flushing until nearly stepped upon. Dozens can be seen at eastern refuges in North Carolina like Mattamuskeet, Pocosin Lakes, and Alligator River, or at boggy protected areas in South Carolina like Santee Coastal Reserve or Donnelley WMA. When flushed, escapes in distinctively erratic flight, calling an explosive *SKRAYT*.

Compact body, short yellow-green legs. Very long bill and long face. Richly patterned with barred sides, striped head and back.

American Woodcock

Scolopax minor

L 11″ | **WS** 18″

Common year-round but not often encountered, the American Woodcock is exceptionally strange for a shorebird. Primarily nocturnal, birds spend the day roosting in hardwood forests, where their dappled plumage makes them nearly impossible to find. At night they travel to wet meadows and pastures to probe for earthworms. Typically encountered by birders when accidentally flushed from underfoot or in late winter, when they can be caught performing their elaborate dusk display in woodland-bordered fields. Male woodcocks strut about with tail fanned like little turkeys calling a buzzy *peeent*, then rocketing into the sky on whistling wings before plummeting back to earth.

Strangely proportioned. Round, short-tailed, with a very long bill. Eye large and set near the top of the head. Buffy on the breast and belly, intricately patterned on the back.

Razorbill

Alca torda

L 17" | **WS** 26"

The chunky, thick-billed Razorbill is the only commonly occurring member of its family, the penguin-like alcids, in the Carolinas. Thousands overwinter in the waters off the coast, often just out of sight, but individuals and small groups can consistently be seen from shore from piers or around inlets. Good spots include Jeanette's Pier in Nags Head and Masonboro Inlet in North Carolina, and Huntington Beach State Park in South Carolina. Razorbills ride low in the water, frequently diving. They fly close to the surf, like black and white footballs with rapid wingbeats.

Long-bodied and distinctly bicolored. Sits low in the water. Thick bill, black and white head with white curling behind eye. Often very active, throwing wings out when diving.

Bonaparte's Gull

Chroicocephalus philadelphia

L 13" | **WS** 31"

This delicate, long-winged gull is a common winter resident of nearshore waters and larger reservoirs throughout the Carolinas. The Bonaparte's Gull is most often seen in flight; its buoyant, tern-like wingbeats and small size distinguish it from other, heftier gulls. It floats over the surface of the water, carefully picking at small pieces of food on the surface with its small, straight bill. Not hard to find anywhere near the ocean from November to April, but particularly abundant around Cape Hatteras, North Carolina, where large flocks can be scrutinized for rarer small gulls.

Immature birds with black wing edges, black M on shoulders. Black-tipped tail.

Small, slender, long-winged. Adult nonbreeding with distinctive white leading edge of wing. Pale gray back, small black dot behind eye. Slender black bill. Flesh-colored legs. Head entirely black in breeding plumage, seen in late spring.

Laughing Gull

Leucophaeus atricilla

L 16" | **WS** 40"

A ubiquitous sight and sound on every beach in the Carolinas during summer, the Laughing Gull is a sharp-looking gull in its breeding finery with jet-black head and blood-red bill. The most common breeding gull in both states, it nests in colonies on small marshy islands and forages on salt water and, increasingly, on freshwater lakes and ponds near the coast. Abundant in summer, the species increasingly lingers through the winter, particularly in South Carolina. Uncommon at larger lakes in late summer and fall. The raucous calls are a pervasive part of the summer beach soundtrack, typically a single brassy *e YAW*, but adults let loose with a loud descending cackle.

Medium-sized and slender, with dark gray back and black wingtips. Adult breeding birds with velvety black head, white eye arcs, and deep red bill and legs.

immature birds with slate gray body, black wingtips. White face with dark wash on the back of the neck. Black bill and legs.

In flight, shows very little white on wingtips. Winter adults with smudgy black marks on back of head. Black bill and legs.

Ring-billed Gull

Larus delawarensis

L 18" | **WS** 44"

If there is one superlative example of a "seagull," it is this omni-present bird of parking lots, fast food joints, and lakeshores. Generally not picky about habitat, so long as there's food and water, they outnumber all other gull species in the Carolinas, particularly inland. Middle-sized with a relatively small bill, the Ring-billed Gull is a useful standard against which to compare the size of larger white-headed gulls and smaller Bonaparte's Gulls. Most common from November through April, but young non-breeding birds linger though the summer months. Call a wheezy *ha-EEEEEE-eee-eee-ee-e*.

Medium-sized, white-headed gull. Pale gray back, black wingtips with small white spots, bright yellow legs. Bill yellow with thick black band towards the end. In winter, often with brown streaks on the nape.

Younger birds blotched brown and gray on back. Bicolored bill, pink at the base and black at the tip. Black tail band. Pink legs.

Herring Gull

Larus argentatus

L 25" | **WS** 56"

Robustly built with a heavy bill, the Herring Gull is the most common large gull along the coast, outnumbered only by the smaller Ring-billed Gull. At its greatest abundance in winter, it is expanding as a breeding bird around the Outer Banks, to the detriment of the terns and shorebirds whose nests it pillages. Herring Gulls are most common in salt water and tidal habitats, often loafing near fishing boats, bait shops, and fish-cleaning stations looking for an easy meal. Regular at larger reservoirs in the Piedmont, but greatly outnumbered by Ring-billed Gulls there. Herring Gulls have a wide variety of keening calls, from the classic ringing *keyeeer* cry to a throaty chuckling *gar-gar-gar-gar*.

Robust, with large head. Heavy yellow bill with red spot towards the tip in adults. Pale gray back, wings with black tips. Pink legs. Extensive brown streaks on head and neck in winter.

Young birds extremely variable, but typically smudgy brown all over. Bill bicolored, increasingly pale as bird ages. Black wingtips, legs pink.

Lesser Black-backed Gull

Larus fuscus

L 21″ | **WS** 54″

Formerly rare visitors from Europe, Lesser Black-backed Gulls have dramatically increased in the Carolinas in the last 20 years. Present on beaches from September through April, it is most easily found in the vicinity of Cape Point on Hatteras Island, North Carolina, where dozens or hundreds congregate in large mixed gull flocks. Nearly every gull flock of decent size in either state can include this species, however, and the slate-gray-backed adults stand out readily among pale-backed Herring and Ring-billed Gulls. Rare, but increasing, at large reservoirs and landfills inland.

Large and slender. Adult (above) with dark gray back, black wingtips with small white spots. Bright yellow legs. Winter birds of any age typically smudgy around the eye. Young birds (right) Palest on head and breast, with some smudgy marks around eye. Bill black. Checkerboard pattern on the back more well-defined than in smudgy young Herring Gull.

Great Black-backed Gull

Larus marinus

L 30" | **WS** 60"

Hulking and massive, with a very heavy bill, the Great Black-backed Gull is the world's largest gull species, and it carries itself as if it knows it. Like the Herring Gull, this species has been increasing as a breeding bird on the Outer Banks, but it is most common in both states in the colder months. Almost always in saltwater or brackish environments, it is tolerant in its food preferences, wolfing down anything it can fit in its mouth. They have even been known to attack and drown waterfowl. Hard to miss anywhere along the coast, it is rare at large reservoirs and landfills inland. Calls are husky growls and low cackles.

assive, with huge head and large bill. Eye looks small.
dult (above) with entirely black back, black wingtips
th large white spots. Bill yellow with red spot towards
e tip. Pink legs. Mostly white-headed year-round.
ung bird (right) with nearly entirely white head, large
ack bill. Well-defined checkerboard pattern on back.
nk legs.

Black Tern

Chlidonias niger

L 10″ | **WS** 24″

Primarily a fall migrant in the Carolinas, the delicate and attractive Black Tern is fairly common to uncommon across both states from July through September. Black Terns don't dive, but rather pick items off the surface of the water. Most common along the coast; the marshes at Pea Island NWR in NC and Bear Island in SC are great places to find them, and they are annual on larger reservoirs in the Piedmont in fall. Many migrate far out to sea, and tropical storms that make landfall in the Carolinas can drive dozens or hundreds inland. Call note is a squeaky chirp.

Late summer migrants (above) often mostly black, speckled with white as they molt. Fairly small, with long wings, dark above and below. Nonbreeding birds (left) with dusky patches around eye, white breast and belly, but variable.

Least Tern

Sternula antillarum

L 9" | **WS** 20"

The tiny, frantic Least Tern is a fairly common breeder along
the coast of both Carolinas and isn't hard to find on any beach
in either state. Nests primarily on beaches and at inlets, and
is sensitive to disturbance by predators, humans, and vehicles,
but diligent protection of nesting colonies has led to a general
increase in the population in recent years. Flight is distinctively
rapid and stiff as it forages in the surf, often quite close to the
beach, diving for small fish in shallow water. Least Terns arrive
on territory in the Carolinas in April and head south fairly
early in fall, with almost all birds gone by the end of September.
Rare inland, usually blown in by storms. Breeding colonies are
loud; calls are hoarse squeaks and chirps.

Very small and slender. Bright yellow bill. Wings
extend well past tail. Black cap, white forehead. In
flight, wings slender, with thin dark leading edge.
Head looks large, bill bright yellow.

Common Tern

Sterna hirundo

L 14" | **WS** 30"

The classic tern across the Northern Hemisphere, the svelte, sickle-winged Common Tern is a local and uncommon breeding bird along the coast and an uncommon migrant elsewhere. Common Terns typically forage well offshore, and are most commonly seen loafing at inlets with other terns or shuttling back and forth between the ocean and nesting colonies on dredge islands or inlets. Similar to the more common Forster's Tern, Common Terns average grayer, with a deeper red bill. Can be seen on the Outer Banks or around Huntington Beach in South Carolina. Can be found on inland lakes and reservoirs in fall, but generally outnumbered by Forster's Terns everywhere. Calls include a squeaky *pik pik pik* and a rattled *keyrrrrrrr*.

Medium-sized, slender and torpedo-shaped. Breeding bird (left) with grayish wash on the body, which sets off white cheeks, black cap. Red bill with smallish black tip. Back and wings gray, darker at the tips. Long forked tail. Nonbreeding bird (top) with black bill, wing tips. Half cap goes around head. Black bar at the shoulder.

Forster's Tern

Sterna forsteri

L 13″ | **WS** 31″

Long-tailed and graceful, the Forster's Tern is the medium-sized tern birders in the Carolinas are most likely to encounter, and the only one that lingers through the winter months. Year-round residents along the coast, Forster's Terns nest in extensive marshes around Pamlico Sound and in the Savannah and Santee River Basins. They tend to forage closer inshore than the similar Common Terns, and are more likely to be found over freshwater as well. In late summer and fall, migrants turn up on large reservoirs and lakes in the Piedmont. Vocalizations are varied, including a hoarse descending *peeerrrr*.

Medium-sized, full-breasted. Very long tail. Breeding birds have orange bill with fairly large black tip. Pale gray back and pale wingtips. Extensive black cap. Nonbreeding birds with black bill, black eye patches with pale nape. Back pale gray and wingtips almost entirely white. Long tail.

Caspian Tern
Hydroprogne caspia

L 20″ | **WS** 45″

Very robust, with a large carrot-orange bill, the Caspian Tern is an uncommon year-round resident and common migrant in the Carolinas. In flight, with broad wings and short tail, it more closely resembles a gull than a tern. It breeds locally on the coast, notably at Oregon Inlet in North Carolina and Huntington Beach State Park in South Carolina, but feeds almost exclusively over fresh or brackish water, like the impoundments at Pea Island NWR. In both states, Caspian Tern is most regularly seen in fall migration, where it stops over every year on larger lakes and reservoirs. Call is harsh and grating, very unlike the squeals and chirps of other terns.

Large, thick-set body. Massive dark red bill. Pale back with slightly darker wingtips. Breeding adults (above) with full cap most of the year. Long, broad-based wings. Thick body, short tail. Nonbreeding adults in winter (left) with speckled black forehead.

Royal Tern

Thalasseus maxima

L 18″ | **WS** 50″

With its large yellow-orange bill and shaggy crest, Royal
Tern cuts a rakish figure on beaches and inlets. It is the most
common large tern on Carolina beaches in the summer months,
with a few lingering through the winter, especially in the south.
Strictly coastal, Royal Terns hunt over salt water, a useful
distinction from the slightly larger Caspian Tern, which prefers
freshwater. The black-capped breeding plumage is held for
only a very short time. Most of the year they appear with a
receding "hairline," with white forehead and crown. Call a
chirpy *kurrrick*.

Large-bodied and long. Shaggy crest.
Most of the year with black half-cap.
Bright orange bill. Pale gray back,
Dark gray to black wingtips.

Entirely black cap held very
briefly in spring. Wings long
and thin at the base
compared to Caspian Tern,
tail more deeply forked.

Sandwich Tern
Thalasseus sandvicensis

L 15" | **WS** 34"

Very pale, with a distinctive yellow-tipped bill, the Sandwich Tern is a common breeding bird on the coast of the Carolinas. Very much like a small version of the Royal Tern, right down to the shaggy crest. The two species are often seen together, nesting in the same colonies; both prefer salt water, with the Sandwich Tern typically foraging closer inshore than the larger Royal. Common along the coast from April through October, but does not overwinter in significant numbers. Call high and grating *teddeeck*.

Medium-sized, slender. Black bill with yellow tip. Pale gray back and wings. Wingtips mostly white, with some black in late summer.

Breeding bird with full cap, long black bill with yellow tip. Shaggy crest. White wingtips. Cap recedes in late summer and fall.

Gull-billed Tern

Gelochelidon nilotica

L 14″ | **WS** 34″

Ghostly pale with an unusually thick, black bill, the Gull-billed Tern is a locally common, but declining, breeding bird in the Carolinas. While most terns dive for small fish in the surf, Gull-billed is highly unusual in that it hunts in dunes and salt marshes, plucking reptiles, small crabs, and insects from vegetation or right off the ground. Present from April through September, Gull-billed Terns can be found on the Outer Banks or around Fort Fisher in North Carolina, or at Huntington Beach and Folly Beach in South Carolina. Call a swingy *per-UP*, similar to Laughing Gull.

Medium-sized, back almost white. Thick, black bill. Short, forked tail. Black cap.

Black Skimmer

Rynchops niger

L 18″ | **WS** 44″

There is no bird in the Carolinas, or in North America, quite like the Black Skimmer. When feeding, it drops the bottom part of its incredible underbite bill into the water, snapping it shut when it intercepts a small fish. With long wings and languid wingbeats, skimmers look as much like pterodactyls as they do their close relatives, the terns. Like many beach-nesting species, Black Skimmers are declining across their range, but they can still be found in moderate numbers anywhere along the coast from April through October, particularly near breeding colonies around Oregon and Mason Inlets in North Carolina and near Folly Beach and Huntington Beach in South Carolina. Less common in winter. Vocalizations are typically variations on a nasal yelp.

Large and sharply bicolored. Very long wings. Large red bill with black tip, lower mandible longer than upper. Entirely black back, wings, and hood.

Tern-like, with short legs an huge bill. Sexes alike in plumage at all ages.

Rock Pigeon

Columba livia

L 13″ | **WS** 25″

The familiar "city pigeon" of urban and agricultural areas
is common throughout the Carolinas and almost exclusively
tied to human habitation. Colors range from the classic gray
with black spots on the wings to an array of browns, blacks,
and whites. Plump with a small head; identification is fairly
straightforward when perched on the ground or on a power line.
Flight is fast and direct, on pointed wings with quick, strong
wingbeats, at times recalling a falcon or gull. Most common in
cities, but often seen in the vicinity of highway overpasses in
rural areas, where they nest in the artificial concrete caverns
underneath, or around grain silos. Normal calls are a series of
bubbling coos.

Plump, with a small head,
tiny bill. "Natural" form is
gray with black wing bars,
iridescence on neck.

Eurasian Collared-Dove
Streptopelia decaocto

L 13″ | **WS** 20″

The latest non-native species to establish a foothold in the
Carolinas, the gentle-looking Eurasian Collared-Dove is a
relatively recent arrival in North America. Widespread along
the coast of South Carolina in tree-lined beachfront surburbs,
less common and local in North Carolina as far north as
Ocracoke Island. Occasionally found around farms with leaky
grain silos. Likely to continue to increase throughout both
states. Prefers to sit up high, on power lines and in the tops of
trees. Song is a breathy *hoo HOOO hoop*.

Medium-sized and full-chested.
Pale sandy brown. Long tail. Small
head and small bill. Small black
half-collar on nape of neck. From
underneath, tail shows a broad
white band at the tip.

Mourning Dove

Zenaida macroura

L 12″ | **WS** 16″

Among the most widespread species in the Carolinas, the sleek, long-tailed Mourning Dove can be found in just about any habitat, from beachfront dunes to cypress swamps to the highest mountains. Plump, small-headed, and perpetually alert, they do best in slightly open places like farms, woodland edges, and residential areas. Flight is usually fast and direct, except when in spring, when males perform a teetering open-winged display glide to attract females. The nests of Mourning Doves are notoriously feeble, a simple pallet of loose sticks on a branch, and summer storms often unceremoniously dump the scaly-plumaged youngsters onto lawns and sidewalks. Feeds mostly on the ground, and flushes with distinctive whistled wingbeats. Song, heard just about everywhere, is a gentle *hooOOO hoo hoo hoo*, like blowing air over a bottle.

ender with a long tail, nall head. Overall warm rown with black spots on ings. Males with bluish idescence on the sides of e neck. White edges on il in flight.

Common Ground-Dove

Columbina passerina

L 6″ | **WS** 10″

Formerly a fairly common breeding bird along the entire coast north to Cape Lookout, now local and declining throughout, the pocket-sized Common Ground-Dove is typically found in dunes and shrubby beach-front thickets along the southern coast of South Carolina. When flushed, flashes striking rufous patches in the wings. Most common between Charleston and the Savannah River, and can be found reliably at Botany Bay WMA, Folly Beach, and the Savannah Spoil Site. Song an abrupt *twoUP twoUP*, repeated at great length.

Sparrow-sized, compact with short tail and legs. Grayish-brown with scaly pattern on head and neck. Black spots on wings. Bill with red base.

Yellow-billed Cuckoo

Coccyzus americanus

L 12″ | **WS** 16″

The lanky, almost serpent-like Yellow-billed Cuckoo is a common, if secretive, breeding bird throughout the Carolinas, present from April through October. Locally, its abundance is greatly tied to outbreaks of tent caterpillars, and cuckoos plunder the hairy larvae with relish in spring. Deliberate in their movements, cuckoos rarely come out into the open, preferring to stay still and hidden in dense cover. When flushed, the Yellow-billed Cuckoo shows surprising rufous patches in the wings and a long tail with large white spots. Most common on the Coastal Plain and or in the Piedmont along rivers and creeks bordered by hardwood forests. Two commonly heard calls, a long clucking *gow-gow-gow-gow-giddup-giddup-giddup* and a more sedate *cdow cdow cdow*.

Long-tailed and gangly. Warm brown on the back with bright white underparts. Large white spots on the underside of the tail. Crisp pattern on the face. Bill mostly yellow. Rufous in the outer flight feathers of the wing.

Black-billed Cuckoo

Coccyzus erythropthalmus

L 12" | **WS** 16"

Secretive, quiet, and easy to overlook, Black-billed Cuckoo is
an uncommon migrant in the Carolinas, and an unpredictable
breeding bird in hardwood forests in the higher mountains
of western North Carolina. Similar to Yellow-billed Cuckoo,
but slightly smaller and generally colder gray; birders should
be wary of dark-billed juvenile Yellow-billed Cuckoos, which
can cause confusion. Black-billed Cuckoos are not reliable
anywhere, but historically the stretches of Blue Ridge Parkway
near Devils Courthouse and Grandfather Mountain have hosted
nesting birds more often than not. They are easiest to find
when vocalizing in July and August, a wooden *too-too-too-too*,
repeated incessantly.

Slender and long-tailed. All-black bill and
red eye ring distinctive. Typically more
gray-brown on upperparts, with buffier
underparts, than Yellow-billed. Small spots
on underside of tail. Wings brown.

Barn Owl

Tyto alba

L 14″ | **WS** 44″

A ghostly presence in coastal marshes and agricultural areas, the Barn Owl's strictly nocturnal habits have made its actual abundance a bit of a mystery. Generally considered an uncommon year-round resident throughout both states, it seems to be declining in the Piedmont and western parts of the Carolinas due to expanding development and the abandonment of old silos and other farm buildings where they prefer to nest. They can still be found along the Coastal Plain, particularly around Pocosin Lakes NWR in North Carolina and Savannah NWR in South Carolina, and a lucky birder out at night might see one in the headlights. Call is an unearthly shriek, as if from the soundtrack of a horror film. Beware the begging calls of young Barred Owls, though, which are very similar.

Medium-sized. Extremely pale, speckled underparts, long legs. Strange monkey-like face. Dark eyes. Sand-colored back and upperwings. Entirely white when seen from below.

Eastern Screech-Owl

Megascops asio

L 8" | **WS** 20-28"

The bark-patterned Eastern Screech-Owl is the smallest of the Carolinas' three commonly occurring owl species. A common, if infrequently encountered, permanent resident throughout both states, these little owls can be found in mixed pine-hardwood forests where they feed on small mammals, large insects, and birds, mostly by night. During the day, Eastern Screech-Owls spend their time roosting in dense trees, vine clumps, and thickets, where they can be very difficult to find. Small perching birds manage to do so fairly regularly, though, and birders can occasionally follow a flock of scolding chickadees, wrens, and titmice to find an annoyed, previously hidden owl. Heard far more often than they are seen, the most common Eastern Screech-Owl vocalizations include a whistled descending whinny and a monotonous bubbly trill. Even poor imitations, made after dark in appropriate habitat, can often elicit a response.

Small, short-tailed, intricately patterned. Large head with short ear tufts, pale eyes. Facial disc bordered with black. Both red and gray morphs are present, but gray form predominates.

Great Horned Owl

Bubo virginianus

L 22" | **WS** 48"

North America's largest owl species, the imposing, column-shaped Great Horned Owl is a fairly common permanent resident in all parts of the Carolinas from barrier islands to the highest mountains. Resilient and adaptable, these massive birds take well to lightly developed areas, broken woodlands, and agricultural areas, where they hunt medium-sized mammals on long, broad wings. Great Horned Owls nest early, with males and females duetting in the cold pre-dawn in December and January and on eggs as early as March. Both sexes' vocalizations include a mellow *hoo, hoo-hoo HOO hoo*, higher pitched in females than in males. Often mobbed by crows and jays during the day; birders can sometimes find roosting owls in the tops of trees by following the ruckus.

Very large, barrel-shaped. Subtly patterned, barred on breast and belly. Often appears as if an extension of a post or tree branch. Yellow eyes, face bordered in black, large ear tufts. Wings long, broad. Head large, blocky. Pale underwings contrast with dark body.

Barred Owl

Strix varia

L 19" | **WS** 42"

The most common owl in the Carolinas year-round, the sad-eyed Barred Owl is active both day and night. They're fond of swampy lowlands, hardwood forests, and even wooded neighborhoods. Typically associated with wet areas, Barred Owls relish frogs, snakes, and crayfish, sometimes dropping right into shallow water in pursuit. The call is a familiar rhythmic barking, often translated as *who COOKS for YOU*, but they also make a variety of barking yelps, some of which sound like monkeys. Young birds make a raspy shriek very much like Barn Owl, though the preferred habitat is wildly different. When flushed from branches in dark woods, Barred Owls look heavy-headed, with stout, rounded wings.

Medium-sized, blocky. Large round head with dark eyes. Mottled brown and white all over. Barring on breast and coarse streaks on belly. Wings fairly stout and round.

Short-eared Owl

Asio flammeus

L 15" **WS** 38"

With their buoyant moth-like flight, seeing Short-eared Owls slowly emerge to hunt over a vast marshy field in winter is a captivating experience. These long-winged open country birds are an uncommon to rare winter visitor on the Coastal Plain, primarily in northeastern North Carolina. Their numbers vary from year to year, generally in response to fluctuating rodent populations in the north, but they are fairly regular along Milltail Road in Alligator River NWR from November through early March. Short-eared Owls begin foraging around sundown, and birders looking to see them should find a field with several Northern Harriers, then wait until the owls begin to replace the harriers as the light fades.

Medium-sized, slender. Long, slightly rounded wings, with large pale patch towards the end. Mottled buff and brown all over, paler on below. Yellow eyes. Very distinct facial disc, yellow eyes surrounded by dark smudges. Mottled back and finely streaked front.

Northern Saw-whet Owl

Aegolius acadicus

L 8″ | **WS** 17″

Tiny, cute, and fierce, the Northern Saw-whet Owl is the smallest species of owl in eastern North America, a fairly common year-round inhabitant of high elevation spruce-fir forests of Appalachian North Carolina and a scattered and secretive winter resident elsewhere. Though they're not rare, saw-whets can be difficult to find because of their small size and retiring habits. When birds are calling in late spring, they can be heard in the Great Smoky Mountains National Park, or along the Blue Ridge Parkway near Mount Mitchell or Grandfather Mountain. Imitating their rhythmic tooting whistle can prompt birds to respond, sometimes even by strafing an unsuspecting birder's head. Their winter distribution is mostly a mystery, but there are scattered records over both states. In recent years, the entrance road at Bodie Island Lighthouse on the Outer Banks has occasionally hosted one or two overwintering birds.

Small, but with a large head. Dark brown back with white spots on shoulders. Coarse brown streaks on light breast and belly. Facial disc buffy, eyes yellow but often closed during the day.

Eastern Whip-poor-will

Antrostomus vociferus

L 10″ | **WS** 19″

Often little more than a disembodied voice ringing from a stand of hardwoods, the Eastern Whip-poor-will is a cryptic, round-headed nocturnal devourer of flying insects. Declining across much of its range in the Carolinas, it seems to take well to clear-cut pine plantations in the Piedmont and Coastal Plain, expanding its range eastward in recent years. Present in the Carolinas from April through September; most often encountered in spring and early summer when singing, a loud, whistled *WHEEper WEEEo*, whence it gets its name, repeated several times.

Cryptic, dark browns and grays. Round-headed, with single central stripe down center of crown. When flushed, male has bright white corners on tail, female buffier.

Chuck-will's-widow

Antrostomus carolinensis

L 12" | **WS** 24"

This large, flat-headed and cryptic member of the goatsucker family is far more often heard than seen. During the day, the Chuck-will's-Widow looks like a richly colored piece of bark as it roosts on the ground in dry pine or mixed pine-hardwood forests in the Coastal Plain and Sandhills regions, or in maritime forests on barrier islands. At night, however, it morphs into an impressive slayer of moths, which it snags with its massive gaped mouth. Fairly common from April through September; birders most often encounter Chuck-will's-widows in spring and early summer, when they can be heard calling an emphatic whistled *tuck-WEEoo-WEEoo* that approximates their name.

Surprisingly big, with a large, flat-crowned head. Intricately camouflaged plumage, mostly rufous. Diffuse streaking on the crown. Looks like an accipiter when flushed, with long wings, tail. White in spread tail up to base.

Common Nighthawk

Chordeiles minor

L 9" | **WS** 21"

The charismatic, sickle-winged Common Nighthawk is an uncommon to locally common and declining breeding bird across the entirety of the Carolinas except for the high mountains. Nighthawks often breed in urban areas, laying eggs on the gravel rooftops of older buildings and hawking for nocturnal flying insects attracted to city lights, so there are plenty of opportunities for birders to cross paths with them from April through September, with peak numbers in August and September. They are also locally common in the Sandhills region, especially in areas that have been recently burned. Nighthawks can be found roosting on the ground or along branches, where cryptic plumage makes them nearly invisible, but typically seen in flight, with long wings beating erratically. Call a buzzy nasal *REEEEnn*.

Medium-sized, front heavy. Long, bent-back wings with white band towards the tip. Dense barring underneath appears dark in low light. Males with white chin, female buffy.

Chimney Swift
Chaetura pelagica

L 5″ | **WS** 12″

A familiar chittering presence over cities and towns throughout the Carolinas in the summer, the little Chimney Swift is a dynamic bird, spending almost all the daylight hours airborne chasing flying insects. Few species are so well adapted to life with humans, as swifts now nest almost exclusively in man-made structures, the uncapped chimneys of human residences or in abandoned factory smokestacks, of which there are plenty in North and South Carolina. With their cylinder-shaped body and bowed wings, Chimney Swifts are often called "flying cigars," and they're often very vocal as small groups course overhead, the bubbly chatter revealing their presence even when very high. In late summer and fall, large flocks congregate in preparation to migrate at communal roosts in large smokestacks, funneling in to roost at sundown like a living tornado of birds.

Small, with cigar-shaped body. Entirely dark. Wings crescent-shaped. Flight fast and acrobatic with quick fluttering wingbeats.

Ruby-throated Hummingbird

Archilochus colubris

L 4″ | **WS** 5″

Among the most beloved birds in the Carolinas, the charismatic little Ruby-throated Hummingbird is a common breeding bird throughout. Easily attracted to homes and gardens with a simple sugar-water feeder, these slender, shimmering green hummingbirds are also common around flowering bushes and shrubs, where they are as interested in the visiting insects as the blooming nectar-rich flowers. Ruby-throated Hummingbirds typically arrive in mid-April and depart in October, but they're an increasingly common overwintering bird on the coast as far north as Cape Hatteras, primarily at feeders. Call is a short sweet tick or a squeaky metallic chatter.

Females and young birds are similar. Plain green on crown and back, white chin, breast, and belly. Pale gray-green on flanks. Tail is often fanned to reveal white spots in the corners.

Very small, almost insect-like, with a needle-like bill. Breeding male (right) with iridescent green crown and back. Dark throat glows blood-red in the right light. Green vest on flanks and forked tail.

Rufous Hummingbird

Selasphorus rufus

L 4″ | **WS** 4.5″

In recent decades, the stocky, pugnacious Rufous Hummingbird has become an increasingly expected winter resident across the Southeast. In the past, birders would remove their hummingbird feeders in October after Ruby-throats depart, but it was soon discovered that those who left them up would occasionally see a different sort of hummingbird, short-tailed with an orange wash on the flanks, arriving a few weeks later. Now dozens to hundreds of Rufous Hummingbirds arrive in the Carolinas every winter, many of them young birds, taking up residence at feeders across both states. The Rufous is a hardy little hummer, breeding as far north as Alaska, and very capable of handling the relatively mild winters of the Southeast. While Rufous is the most likely "different" hummer, birders should note that 12 species of hummingbird have been recorded in the Carolinas.

More compact than Ruby-throated, with a shorter bill. Immature birds with rufous wash on the flanks and green back and head. When tail is fanned, feathers are rufous at base. Adult males uncommon, but unmistakable. Copper-penny body, with red throat.

Belted Kingfisher
Megaceryle alcyon

L 13" | **WS** 20"

With its dashing crest and dagger bill, the charismatic Belted Kingfisher is an exciting permanent resident on almost every body of water in the Carolinas short of the open ocean. Kingfishers often make their presence known by bursting onto the scene with an explosive ratcheting call, perching on a limb overhanging the water, or hurtling downriver out of sight. They nest in burrows excavated in muddy vertical cliffs on or near rivers, and are relatively reserved during this time of the year, before returning with a vengeance in late summer. Kingfishers capture fish in spectacular plunge dives, from a limb or power line or after hovering in mid-air over still water. Most common in winter, when resident numbers are augmented by migrants from the north.

Large head, with a long, straight gray bill. Blue-gray above and mostly white below. Shaggy crest and white collar. Blue breast band. Female (shown) has a rusty belly band that males lack.

Red-headed Woodpecker

Melanerpes erythrocephalus

L 9″ | **WS** 17″

The Red-headed Woodpecker, strikingly patterned and gregarious, is a fairly common year-round resident in open woodlands across the Carolinas. Family groups occupy mature pine and hardwood forests and even manicured areas like cemeteries and parks, provided the tree cover is not too dense. In winter, they are particularly fond of swampy areas like impoundments and beaver ponds with large standing snags, which family groups use as acorn larders. It is not a common visitor to feeders away from such places. Groups are vocal, making various coarse rolling *CHURRRs* and burry chatters.

Medium-sized. Solid red head. Black back with large white patch on inner wing. White belly. Immature birds with dingy gray head. White wing patch barred. Scaly back.

Red-bellied Woodpecker

Melanerpes carolinus

L 9″ **WS** 16″

A common woodpecker throughout with a flashy zebra-striped back, the Red-bellied Woodpecker is hard to miss in a typical day's birding anywhere in the Carolinas. Red-bellieds are widespread in all types of forests and edge habitats, though they seem to prefer hardwoods. They're also common visitors to residential feeding stations that offer sunflower seeds or suet. Shows the "woodpecker bounce" in flight, bursts of wing-beats interspersed with longish glides in a distinctive wavy pattern. The most commonly given vocalizations include a rich *CHEW!*, given singly or as part of a descending chuckle, and a rolling *qurrrrrrrra*.

Medium-sized, with densely barred back. Tan face and belly. Male with red crown and nape. In female, red is restricted to nape. White rump in flight.

Yellow-bellied Sapsucker

Sphyrapicus varius

L 8″ | **WS** 16″

If you've ever seen a neat row of small holes in the bark of a tree, then you're familiar with the work of the Yellow-bellied Sapsucker. The Yellow-bellied Sapsucker is a scattered breeding bird in the high mountains of western North Carolina and a common winter resident elsewhere. The small holes it methodically drills in tree trunks and limbs leak sap, which the woodpecker then eats. The holes are also important early spring food sources for insects and small birds. In winter, sapsuckers often travel in mixed flocks with chickadees, titmice, and wrens. Call is a nasal squeal, like a whining cat.

Medium-sized, adult with boldly patterned head. Red on crown. Male with red chin bordered in black, female's chin white. Mostly black wings with large white slash on the side. White rump. Grayish belly with indistinct barring. Immature birds with ashy head. Large white slash in the wing.

Downy Woodpecker

Picoides pubescens

L 7" | **WS** 12"

The smallest woodpecker in the Carolinas, the chubby, short-billed Downy Woodpecker is a common year-round resident across both states and a regular visitor to feeders. More than most woodpeckers, Downies are capable of thriving in a wide variety of habitats, and their small size allows them to forage in second-growth forest, along wooded edges, and on small-diameter trees or towards the thin edges of branches. In winter, often joins roving flocks of chickadees, titmice, and wrens, lightly tapping on branches as the birds swarm about. Calls include a mellow *teek!*, like a small pet toy, and a descending squeaky rattle.

Fairly small, bicolored. Small bill. Black cheek. Mostly black upperparts spotted with white on the wings, rectangular white patch in the middle of the back. Male has small patch of red on the nape.

Hairy Woodpecker

Picoides villosus

L 9″ | **WS** 15″

The natty, medium-sized Hairy Woodpecker is an uncommon permanent resident throughout the state, though generally more common in the western third of the Carolinas. They are less likely to show up at feeders in residential areas than other woodpeckers, preferring more extensive hardwood and mixed forests with larger trees. Though similar to the smaller Downy Woodpecker, the bill is significantly larger, nearly the same length as the head, clearly different from the tiny tack-sized chisel of the smaller bird. Calls include a sharp *CHEEK!*, as in a forceful squeeze of a dog toy, and a sputtery rattle.

Medium-sized, sharply black and white. Bill long and heavy. Black cheek. Black wings with white spots, white rectangle on back. Male with red spot on nape.

Red-cockaded Woodpecker

Picoides borealis

L 8″ | **WS** 14″

An endangered species with very specific habitat requirements, the Red-cockaded Woodpecker is actually fairly common where it does occur. No species in the Carolinas is more closely tied to frequently burned stands of pine, typically longleaf, and they readily take to open pine forests with grassy understory. Unlike any other North American woodpecker, Red-cockaded excavates nesting cavities in living trees, drilling small holes around the nest entrance to induce sap flow and create a sticky border protecting the eggs from snakes and squirrels. Because of this, the white and shiny active nest trees are easy to find, even more so because state and federal agencies usually mark them with thick white bands around the trunk. Good places to see them include Croatan National Forest, Sandhills Game Lands, and Weymouth Woods Preserve in NC, and Carolina Sandhills NWR or Francis Marion National Forest in SC. Family groups are chatty, giving a bubbling series of rubber duck squeaks.

Relatively small, with round head and bright white cheek patch. Back entirely black with white specks. Underside white with black specks.

Northern Flicker

Colaptes auratus

L 12" | **WS** 20"

A most unusual woodpecker, clad in speckled brown instead of black and white, the Northern Flicker is a common permanent resident in the Carolinas. More than other woodpeckers, they prefer open woodlands, forest edges, and pastures, often foraging for insects and earthworms on the ground. When flushed from the ground, flickers show a white rump and flashy yellow patches in the wings, thus, the name "Yellow-shafted" given to the birds in eastern North America. Sociable and vocal; typical calls include a sharp *PEEuck*, a rapid *kyu-kyu-kyu-kyu-kyu*, and a squealing *WEEK-a WEEK-a WEEK-a*.

Fairly large and long-bodied. Large, black, slightly curved bill. Tan with black bars on the wings and spots on belly. Black chest. Gray crown and nape with small red spot on back of head. Male with black moustache. Female with plain brown face. Both sexes show bright yellow feathers in flight, obvious white rump.

Pileated Woodpecker

Dryocopus pileatus

L 16" | **WS** 29"

Easily one of the most spectacular birds in the Carolinas, this impressive woodpecker with a jaunty red crest is a fairly common permanent resident throughout both states. Pileated Woodpeckers are typically found in more extensive hardwood forests with larger trees, particularly in the Coastal Plain, but occasionally make their way into well-forested neighborhoods. Large size is apparent in flight; deep rowing wingbeats with white below, and little of the bouncing rhythm of smaller woodpeckers. Typical call a far-reaching, resonant *kuk-kuk-kuk-kuk-kuk-kuk-kuk*.

Impressively large. Entirely black back, boldly striped face and neck, and shocking red crest are unmistakable. Female has black forehead. In flight, note broad wings with large white patches on underwing.

American Kestrel

Falco sparverius

L 9" | **WS** 22"

Lithe and colorful, the American Kestrel is the most wide-spread falcon in the Carolinas. It's a fairly common year-round resident of open spaces and pastures, and can often be seen perched in a prominent location like power lines and the bare branches atop dead trees, where it bobs its tail while searching for large insects and small mammals below. In flight it has long, pointed wings and a long tail and graceful, bounding wingbeats; often hovers while hunting. Most common on the Coastal Plain, where several per day can still be seen, and less common westward as open country gives way to development and unbroken forests. When disturbed, lets loose with a ringing *klee-klee-klee-klee-klee!*

Small and slight, with long tail and wings. Male (left)colorful with blue wings, red back, boldly patterned head, spotted and barred throughout. Tail with black tip. Female (below) less colorful, mostly rufous with coarse streaking on breast, barred tail. In flight, wings are long and thin. Underparts mostly pale. Head relatively small.

Merlin

Falco columbarius

L 10″ | **WS** 24″

Burly and aggressive, the Merlin is a small falcon with the attitude of a much bigger bird. Most common in the Carolinas as a fall migrant, fair numbers of these stocky raptors can be seen migrating down the coast in September and October and elsewhere in the state in much lower numbers. A few over-winter in the eastern third of both states, and can typically be found at places like Pea Island NWR or Santee Coastal Reserve, where wintering shorebirds congregate. When perched, Merlins like an unobstructed view; you can find them on snags, power poles, and crossbars, but rarely on the wires like kestrels.

Small but solidly built, bull-necked with a relatively large head. Dark gray back and wings. Wings broad-based and relatively short. Checkerboard underwing pattern.

Peregrine Falcon

Falco peregrinus

L 16″ | **WS** 41″

The Peregrine Falcon was extirpated from the eastern half of the continent in the middle of last century, so it's always a treat to see this powerful raptor once again nesting in the North Carolina mountains. Peregrines nest on vertical cliffs in the Linville Falls, Chimney Rock, and Devils Courthouse area, and can be seen year-round there. Charlotte and Winston-Salem also have semi-resident birds on large buildings downtown; they've nested there in the past, and may do so again. Elsewhere in the Carolinas, they're uncommon fall migrants, peaking in October, and winter residents towards the coast, most easily seen at places where waterfowl and shorebirds congregate.

Fairly large, with a rounded head and barrel-shaped body. Very long wings. Adults dark gray on back, with pale breast and finely barred belly. Dark hood.. Bright yellow around eye and base of bill. Wings wid at base and sharply pointe Finely barred underneath, appears pale.

Acadian Flycatcher

Empidonax virescens

L 6″ | **WS** 9″

Small and nondescript, the Acadian Flycatcher is a conspicuous breeding bird in hardwood bottomland forests of the Carolinas. The most common and widespread member of the occasionally mystifying genus *Empidonax*, Acadian Flycatchers are most often heard before they're seen, their typical song a curt *pet-SWEET!*, often accompanied by squeaky titters. Present from mid-April through October, but most conspicuous in spring and early summer when singing. Prefers broadleaf forests, usually near creeks or rivers.

Small and compact, with large, slightly peaked head. Green on back and head with a large eye ring and two bold wing bars. Mostly pale chin, breast, and belly, but fall birds can look yellowish.

Least Flycatcher

Empidonax minimus

L 5″ | **WS** 8″

The tiny, short-winged Least Flycatcher is the smallest flycatcher in eastern North America, and most distinctive of the *Empidonax* flycacthers. With its large eyes and tiny beak, Least Flycatcher is objectively "cute" in appearance and demeanor, as it hunts small insects in shrubby second-growth forests, overgrown pastures, or along the edges of the woods, frequently twitching its wings. Fairly common, but localized, breeding birds in the mountains of North Carolina and the western tip of South Carolina, they prefer middle elevations from 3000 to 4500 feet. Elsewhere, they're an uncommon migrant, mostly in fall. Song a tinny *TSEEbek*, often repeated.

Very small and cute. Eye looks large on round head, bill short. Bold eye ring. Wings very short.

Alder Flycatcher

Empidonax alnorum

L 6" | **WS** 8.5"

The Alder Flycatcher is a scattered breeding bird of bogs and swampy seeps above 3,500 feet in elevation. A late migrant, they usually don't arrive on territory until nearly June, and can be conspicuous for about a month at places like Mount Mitchell State Park or Roan Mountain as they establish territories. Distinctive song is a buzzy rising *trrrrBEETa*, sometimes written as *free beer!* Similar in many respect to other *Empidonax* flycatchers, particularly Willow, so silent birds away from known sites should be identified with care, or simply left unidentified.

Very similar to Willow Flycatcher, but with a more rounded head. Bold wing bars. Color more green than gray on head and back, pale underneath. Very thin eye ring.

Willow Flycatcher

Empidonax traillii

L 6" | **WS** 8.5"

The Willow Flycatcher is an uncommon and local breeding bird in the western half of North Carolina, and a rare migrant elsewhere. As the name suggests, they generally nest in streamside thickets (often with willows), overgrown pastures, or tree-lined marshes, below 3,000 feet in elevation. Like the Alder Flycacther, the Willow is a late migrant, arriving in the Carolinas in mid-May. In appearance, virtually identical to Alder Flycatcher, best differentiated in summer by breeding location and vocalizations. Willow's song is a ripping *BRRREE-chew*, the call a liquid *whit*.

Very similar to Alder Flycatcher, but crown peaked more towards the back of the head. Eye ring very thin, sometimes appears absent. More gray than green, pale underneath. Bold wing bars, wings relatively short.

Eastern Wood-Pewee

Contopus virens

L 6″ | **WS** 10″

A familiar and beloved voice in the woods, the Eastern Wood-Pewee is a common breeding bird in almost any forest throughout the states. Arriving in the Carolinas in mid-April, pewees make their presence known immediately with their tipsy whistled *BEE-yo-WEE*, or the abbreviated version *BEE-yo*. Often perch fairly high on exposed twigs, sallying out after insects and returning to the original perch with a little shudder. Often active throughout the day, and hard to miss at the right time of year in the right habitat. Leaves the Carolinas abruptly in mid-October.

Fairly small and indistinct. Plain face with no eye ring. Gray-brown all over, with dusky wash on breast. Slightly peaked head, two thin wing bars on very long wings.

Eastern Phoebe

Sayornis phoebe

L 7" | **WS** 10"

The Eastern Phoebe is a stout, large-headed flycatcher commonly associated with human habitation, nesting under eaves and on exposed beams on houses, farm buildings, and bridges. They are common year-round across most of the Carolinas, but known only as a wintering bird in the eastern third of the states. The Eastern Phoebe can be found in nearly any sort of open area, including golf courses, marshes, parks, and yards, where it perches fairly low, regularly and deliberately bobbing its tail. Song is a familiar *BEE-perrr* or *BEE-pit-it*, whence its name.

Medium-sized, full-chested. Dark gray on back and darker on the head. No wing bars or eye ring. Smudgy on side of the breast. Birds in winter often shows yellow wash on underparts.

Great Crested Flycatcher

Myiarchus crinitus

L 9" | **WS** 13"

Lanky and pugnacious, the Great Crested Flycatcher is a
common, and often conspicuous, breeding bird across the
Carolinas. Most numerous in the Coastal Plain and the Piedmont,
they are our only cavity-nesting flycatcher, preferring forests
with mature trees and large snags, but occasionally finding
appropriate spots in well-wooded neighborhoods, too. Typically
staying in the upper branches, they are heard more than they
are seen, making their presence known with an emphatic rising
WEEEP or a series of burry *brrrt brrrt* calls. Present from April
through September, apparent Great Crested Flycatchers out of
season are potentially the similar Ash-throated Flycatcher, a
rare but regular winter visitor on the Coastal Plain.

Robin-sized, with a big, peaked head. Large
dark bill. Yellow wash on belly. Brownish on
back and wings, darker on head. Gray
breast, rufous flashes in wings and tail.

Eastern Kingbird

Tyrannus tyrannus

L 9" | **WS** 15"

The the smartly patterned Eastern Kingbird, noisy and conspicuous, is fairly common from April through early October in open country throughout the region. Most common in the eastern half of the Carolinas, Eastern Kingbirds can often be seen perched on power lines and fences near pastures, marshes, and forest edges, usually in an area with a few scattered trees where they can nest. Notably aggressive, they escort raptors and other larger birds out of their territory with extreme prejudice, diving and chittering at them the whole way. Call is a series of manic chirpy *zzeet zzet zzeet* buzzes often strung together, like the scrape of a branch on a car door.

Medium-sized, conspicuously bicolored. Bold white band at end of tail. Head slightly peaked, bill quite large. Black upperparts and white below. Gray wash on breast.

Loggerhead Shrike
Lanius ludovicianus

L 9″ | **WS** 12″

The seemingly innocuous, even cute, appearance of the
Loggerhead Shrike conceals a cunning predator of small
mammals, reptiles, and large insects. Known as the "butcher-
bird" for its practice of impaling prey on barbed wire or thorny
shrubs for consumption later, this shrike is an uncommon
permanent resident of open country in the eastern half of the
Carolinas. Sadly, populations of this charismatic bird have
declined significantly in the Piedmont in recent decades, but
they can still be found with some regularity by driving back
roads through the pastures and farmland of the Sandhills and
the Coastal Plain. Song is a slow series of electrical, disyllabic
chirps and buzzes.

Medium-sized. Gray body with
large head and bold black mask.
Stout, black, noticeably hooked
bill. Pale below. Wings and tail
black with white flashes.

White-eyed Vireo

Vireo griseus

L 5″ | **WS** 7.5″

Animated and colorful, with a fierce expression, the White-eyed Vireo is a common and familiar breeding bird in shrubby fields, tree-lined marshes, and dense tangles throughout the Carolinas. Unlike the other vireos in the Carolinas, White-eyes prefer to stay within 15 feet of the ground, usually remaining just out of sight behind a wall of thick vegetation. Generally arriving in the Carolinas in mid-March and departing in mid-October, a handful linger through the winter on the coast, particularly in mild winters. Song is a loud mechanical *chick-purdaWEEER-chick*, written occasionally as *quick, gimme the rain check*, often given from cover.

Fairly small, mostly green with yellow flanks, yellow around bright white eye. Two bold white wing bars, black bill. Young birds in late summer have dark eye.

Yellow-throated Vireo

Vireo flavifrons

L 5.5" | **WS** 9.5"

A classic species of eastern hardwood forests, the sluggish Yellow-throated Vireo is a common breeding bird across most of the Carolinas. Like most vireos, it spends much of its time high in the canopy, moving deliberately and heavily from branch to branch. For most birders its presence is revealed by its song, a series of slow, hoarse two-syllable phrases *VRREE-en … SHEE-o* repeated over and over. Present from April through October, Yellow-throated Vireos can be located without too much trouble at any state park or protected area with extensive broad-leaf forests, particularly in the Piedmont and low mountains.

Medium-sized, with glowing yellow throat and bold "spectacles" around dark eye. Large, stout, hooked bill. Bright white wing bars. Mostly gray on the back, with a bright white belly.

Blue-headed Vireo

Vireo solitarius

L 5.5″ | **WS** 9.5″

Compact and smartly-patterned, the Blue-headed Vireo's distribution in the Carolinas depends on the region. It's a common breeding bird in the western mountains, where it can be found in spruce-fir or mixed forests above 3,000 feet in elevation. Along the coast, it is a fairly common wintering bird, where it joins nomadic mixed flocks of warblers and chickadees in low maritime forests. Elsewhere, it is typically seen in spring and fall, but is also a scattered breeder and uncommon winter resident. The typical song of Blue-headed Vireos is a squeaky series of slurred two- and three-note phrases *SVEE-oh WEE-o-up SVEE-ah*, sounding pinched at the ends of the phrases; the call is a rattling chatter.

Medium-sized, with gray head and bold white "spectacles," white chin. Gray-green body and lime-green flanks. Bright white underneath. Stout black bill. Two white wing bars.

Warbling Vireo

Vireo gilvus

L 5.5″ | **WS** 8.5″

This plain-faced songster reaches the southeastern extreme of its vast range in western North Carolina. Warbling Vireo is a local breeding bird at relatively low elevations in the mountains and scattered throughout the western Piedmont. Elsewhere it is an uncommon migrant, nearly exclusively in the spring. It prefers riverine hardwood forests, particularly in the French Broad and New River valleys, and even when it occurs elsewhere, it is generally near rivers or forested lakes. Song is a rambling rhythmic warble *ververveevoververververvee VEET* and call a peevish whine.

Fairly small, extremely plain. Pattern on face faint. Pale gray-green on back, pale underneath. Yellowish on flanks. No wing bars.

Philadelphia Vireo

Vireo philadelphicus

L 5″ | **WS** 8″

With a cute face and creamy yellow underparts, the Philadelphia Vireo is an exciting find anywhere in the Carolinas. The only eastern vireo that does not nest in either state, they are primarily known as a fall migrant, peaking between September and mid-October and taking a route that takes them mostly through the western Piedmont and the mountains. Can be found in mixed flocks with migrating warblers, following along quietly in the background and easily overlooked. Usually silent in the Carolinas, but song is a series of sing-songy phrases similar to other vireos; call is a nasal *mew*.

Small, cute, with well-defined pattern on face. Dark crown and dark eye line. Yellow underneath, brightest around throat. Gray-green back. No wing bars.

Red-eyed Vireo

Vireo olivaceus

L 6" | **WS** 10"

Its voice the omnipresent soundtrack of the eastern forests, the treetop-dwelling Red-eyed Vireo is a very common breeding bird in nearly all parts of the Carolinas. It is easy to hear, if not see, from April through October in just about any forested landscape, typically working a methodical path through the canopy while singing a series of clear three- to four-part phrases *WHERE are you, HERE I am, SEE me here now,* repeated ad nauseam. On hot summer afternoons, it may be the only species vocalizing. A bit easier to see in fall, when it becomes a fairly conspicuous part of mixed migrating songbird flocks in September and October, even in low maritime forests where it's absent as a breeding bird.

Medium-sized and long-bodied. Bold face pattern, gray cap bordered by black, black eye line. Red eye often appears dark. Green back and wings, pale below with yellowish wash. Bill longer, thinner than in other vireos.

Blue Jay
Cyanocitta cristata

L 11″ | **WS** 16″

Though a familiar sight throughout the Carolinas, the gaudy Blue Jay surely ranks among one of our most beautiful birds. Conspicuous and gregarious, they're a common permanent resident in nearly all forests and well-wooded neighborhoods, particularly those with mature oak trees. Easy to find most of the year, they are particularly evident in fall, when loose flocks drift south over the trees with heavy, inconstant wingbeats. Like most members of the corvid family, they are quite noisy, making a wide variety of squealing, whistling vocalizations and even a fair impersonation of Red-shouldered Hawk. The classic Blue Jay cry is a harsh descending *YAAAY*, often given when harassing raptors.

Boldly patterned face bordered by black. Blue crest raised or lowered at will. Carolina blue on back, darker on wings and tail, with black bars. Thick black bill. Gray breast and belly. White flashes in tail tips.

American Crow
Corvus brachyrhynchos

L 17" | **WS** 39"

Quite possibly the easiest bird to find in the Carolinas, the American Crow is a common and conspicuous permanent resident in a wide variety of habitats. The crow is widely considered to be one of the most intelligent birds in North America, characterized by its versatility and complex social structure. Crows eat nearly anything, from roadkill and garbage to fruits, seeds, and small animals, occasionally raiding the nests of other birds for eggs or chicks. In fall and winter, crows gather in nomadic and noisy flocks, sometimes numbering in the hundreds, in forests, pastures, and landfills. Crows make a wide variety of vocalizations, the most common of which is a harsh *CAW!*, but also including various croaks, rattles, and squawks.

Large, and entirely glossy black. Long, thick bill. In flight, broad rounded wings. Tail fairly short.

Fish Crow

Corvus ossifragus

L 15" | **WS** 36"

Slimmer and glossier than American Crow, the frog-voiced Fish Crow is most common in the Piedmont and Coastal Plain, where it is best differentiated from its slightly larger relative by its call, a nasal *NUH-uh*. Most of the year it isn't hard to find around reservoirs or large rivers in much of the state, but it mostly retreats to the Coastal Plain during the coldest months. Like American Crow, it is versatile and gregarious, but the two species typically do not associate with one another except in places like landfills. Replaces flight feathers later than American Crow, a clue to identifying non-vocalizing birds during a brief period of the year. Birds showing symmetrically missing wing feathers in summer are American Crows, while those showing such a pattern in fall are Fish Crows.

Slightly smaller than American Crow, with shorter legs and longer wings and tail. Differences subtle; best distinguished by voice.

Common Raven

Corvus corax

L 24" | **WS** 46–50"

Appearing more like a raptor than a songbird, the imposing
Common Raven is a common year-round resident in
Appalachian North and South Carolina, where it mostly
replaces crows above 3,000 feet in elevation. In recent years,
this species has been moving eastward into the Piedmont,
and is regularly seen as far east as Raleigh in North Carolina, though oddly it is still restricted to the far west in South
Carolina. Shows typical corvid versatility and intelligence, but
less inclined to flock with smaller crows or even other ravens.
Ravens are typically seen solo or in pairs. In North Carolina,
ravens can be encountered at many spots along the Blue Ridge
Parkway; in South Carolina, Caesar's Head and Sassafras
Mountain are good bets. Call is a gruff rolling *rawk rawk*.

Very large, similar in size to a
large hawk. Glossy black. Very
long wings and large bill.
Shaggy feathers around
throat. Often soars like a
raptor on long wings with
distinct "fingers." Long
wedge-shaped tail, large bill.

Horned Lark
Eremophila alpestris

L 7″ | **WS** 12″

Fairly common year-round in the Carolinas but easy to miss, the furtive Horned Lark is a bird of overgrazed pastures, agricultural fields, and sand dunes. A sporadic nester in both North and South Carolina, it prefers nearly bare ground, where it builds a simple cup nest hidden in a grass tussock. Numbers in winter are augmented by northern migrants, and Horned Larks often gather in large flocks in winter and early spring in large cultivated fields on the Coastal Plain. Its presence is best detected by listening for the vocalizations. The song is a thin tinkling warble, the flight call a thin, descending *peeer*.

Small, sand-colored. Bold face pattern with black mask, small "horns." Dark across breast. Yellow wash on face and breast. Tail dark with white outer feathers.

Purple Martin

Progne subis

L 8″ **WS** 16″

North America's largest swallow, the chatty, broad-winged Purple Martin is a common and beloved breeding bird throughout the Carolinas. Nearly entirely dependent on humans for nesting cavities, this consummate aerialist is most often found in the vicinity of large multi-nest structures and gourd arrays erected by homeowners; the martins pull their weight as voracious predators of insect pests. They take readily to open sites adjacent to pastures or large yards, particularly those near ponds. In fall, stages in spectacular flocks before heading south, and many thousands gather annually to roost beneath the Old Highway 64 bridge to Roanoke Island in North Carolina between mid-July and mid-August. The simultaneous calls of groups of birds produce a bubbling chatter like an active coffee percolator. Individual birds make a rich descending *cheew*.

Large for a swallow. Male (left) glossy purple with darker wings and tail. Small bill. Shallow forked tail. Female (right) with dark head and paler gray belly.

Tree Swallow

Tachycineta bicolor

L 6″ | **WS** 14″

One of the most commonly encountered swallows in the Carolinas, the sharply bicolored Tree Swallow is primarily known as a winter resident and migrant, though it is a sporadic but increasing nester in the mountains. Robust and cold-hardy, Tree Swallows overwinter in massive flocks, sometimes many thousands strong around Pamlico Sound, but occur in smaller numbers elsewhere along the coast. Generally the only swallows to persist into winter, they are able to survive periods of cold weather by switching their diet to wax myrtle berries. Most often seen swooping in lazy circuits over lakes and ponds in late summer and fall in flocks of a dozen or more. Call is an abrupt zipping chirp, given frequently.

Adult male glossy aquamarine on back, darker on wings and tail, bright white underparts. In flight, white underparts contrast with dark underwings. Female gray-brown on top. Tail barely forked, looks square when fanned.

Northern Rough-winged Swallow

Stelgidopteryx serripennis

L 5.5" | **WS** 11"

Dingy and modest, the Northern Rough-winged Swallow is a common breeding bird across the entirety of both states. They require vertical cliff banks in which to excavate their nests, so colonies are fairly local, but they disperse widely to forage, and individuals or small groups can be found on just about any pond, lake, or larger river from March through October. Fairly broad-winged with a short, squared tail, Northern Rough-winged Swallows often call a low *thip thip thip*.

Medium-sized, brown back and head. Indistinct brownish wash across throat and breast. Tail short. Fairly narrow wings, mostly brownish all over with dingy white belly. Square-tipped tail.

Bank Swallow

Riparia riparia

L 5″ | **WS** 13″

Notably dainty and flying with distinctively buzzy, frantic wingbeats, the Bank Swallow is an uncommon migrant in the Carolinas, though it has bred in the past and may do so again in the future. It is present in the Carolinas mostly inland in April and May and again along the coast from mid-July through mid-September, associating with other species of swallows at freshwater ponds, lakes, and reservoirs, where it can be picked out by its small size and gleaming white underparts. Call is very different from other swallows, a croaky *brrrp* or *brr-bip*.

Very small, with narrow wings and a long, forked tail. Bright white on belly and flanks. Brown breast band borders white chin.

Cliff Swallow

Petrochelidon pyrrhonota

L 5.5″ | **WS** 11″

Stocky, with a distinctive pale rump and short square tail, the Cliff Swallow is a fairly common breeding bird in most parts of the Carolinas. Like other swallows, they take readily to man-made structures, building their unique rounded mud nests on the undersides of eaves and, particularly, bridges. Fair-sized colonies can be found around lakes and large rivers in the Piedmont and parts west, arriving in late March and departing fairly early in late summer. Calls a series of husky chirps.

Medium-sized and colorful for a swallow. Navy blue back, buffy belly and breast. Pale nape. Brick red cheek and chin. Blue cap with pale forehead. Broad-based, triangular wings. Pale rump distinctive. Square-tipped tail.

Barn Swallow

Hirundo rustica

L 7" | **WS** 12"

A deft aerialist and the source of the term "swallow-tailed," the slender Barn Swallow is a common and familiar breeding bird across the Carolinas. Barn Swallows are ready adapters of human structures, with colonies building their little mud cup nests under bridges, eaves, and highway overpasses or in barns. Found in just about any open space from March into November, particularly near ponds and lakes. Flight is graceful, with snappy wingbeats and long tail, often appearing as a long single point, trailing behind. Calls include squeaky *zip-zap* and burry rattles.

Medium-sized, very thin and dark. Navy blue back and crown, orange-red chin and underparts. Tail very long. Long, narrow wings. Deeply forked tail with small white spots.

Carolina Chickadee

Poecile carolinensis

L 5″ | **WS** 7.5″

The audacious little Carolina Chickadee is a common permanent resident in a wide variety of forest habitats throughout the Carolinas. It can be a regular visitor to feeders offering sunflower seeds or suet, particularly in wooded neighborhoods. Begins singing quite early in the spring, a plaintive *TSEE-bee tsee-bay*. Calls are typically variations on *psee-dee-chettet* or *chechechecheche*, and small feeding flocks are noisy as they work their way through the forest, exploring every nook and hanging acrobatically from branches to pry out stubborn seeds. A regular component of mixed flocks in fall and winter; seeking out chickadees in fall is often a good strategy for finding more secretive birds. The similar Black-capped Chickadee (*Poecile atricapillus*) is present only above 5,000 feet in the Smoky Mountains in the far west.

mall, round body with a long tail. old pattern on large head. Black ap, neatly bordered throat, white heek. Wings plain gray. Flanks gray.

Tufted Titmouse

Baeolophus bicolor

L 6.5" | **WS** 10"

Noisy, with no shortage of sass, the cute, crested Tufted Titmouse is similar in many respects to its smaller chickadee cousins. All prefer forested habitats, and are eager adopters of feeding stations in wooded neighborhoods, and chickadees and titmice are the hubs around which feeding flocks of perching birds form in fall and winter. Sings almost year-round, a ringing *PEEtaPEEtaPEEtaPEEta* that is hard to miss, particularly in spring. Calls are impressively varied, often a high pitched *seeh seeh seeh* or a *TSEE-shay-shay-shay*.

Fairly small; plain face with large black eye. Small gray crest. Gray all over, darker on back and head than underparts. Orangish wash on flanks. Stout black bill.

Red-breasted Nuthatch

Sitta canadensis

L 4.5″ | **WS** 8.5″

The only nuthatch in the Carolinas with seasonal movements, the dapper little Red-breasted Nuthatch is a common permanent resident in the mountains and an erratic winter visitor elsewhere. Mostly associated with conifers where it occurs, it breeds in spruce-fir stands along the Blue Ridge Parkway in North Carolina and in white pines in the far western tip of South Carolina, where its call, a repetitive nasal *hink hink hink,* confirms its presence. They're rather uncommon throughout the rest of the Carolinas in winter, but they'll occasionally stage "irruptions" into the lowlands, when the striking little birds show up at feeders and pine lots in the Piedmont and parts east.

Small, with large head and short tail. Bold pattern on face. Black cap, white eyebrow, black eye stripe. Gray back. Underparts mostly salmon red, paler in females than males.

White-breasted Nuthatch

Sitta carolinensis

L 6″ | **WS** 11″

The simply-patterned White-breasted Nuthatch cuts a familiar and distinctive figure as it creeps headfirst down the trunk of a large hardwood tree. A widespread and mostly common permanent resident throughout the Carolinas, it's a classic species of the eastern deciduous forest and a regular visitor to bird feeders in wooded neighborhoods. Alongside chickadees and titmice, it's often a core component of mixed flocks in fall and winter, when its call, a pinched *hent hent*, is prevalent.

Medium-sized, with a large head and a long, slightly upturned bill. Black eye on plain white face. Black cap and nape. Gray back, mostly white underparts with gray-buff wash on the flanks. Female similar, with paler cap.

Brown-headed Nuthatch

Sitta pusilla

L 4.5″ | **WS** 8″

Gregarious and noisy, the undeniably cute Brown-headed Nuthatch is a classic species of the southeastern pine flatlands, and a common permanent resident throughout the Piedmont and Coastal Plain. Brown-headed Nuthatches are almost exclusively associated with pine trees, and they're most numerous in mature stands of longleaf pine in the Sandhills. They're less picky than other southeastern pine specialists, though, and also take to edge habitats in neighborhoods, golf courses, and parks with sizable stands of pines. Often forage fairly high, where the small birds can be tough to spot as they bounce among branches, but their distinctive rubber-ducky chatter can't be missed.

Small, short-tailed, with warm brown cap and nape, darker around eye. White chin. Back gray, underparts mostly pale, washed with gray. Long dark bill.

Brown Creeper

Certhia americana

L 5″ | **WS** 8″

Cryptic and shy, the slender Brown Creeper is widespread in the Carolinas but remarkably easy to overlook. Brown Creepers are permanent residents in the higher mountains of western North Carolina, where they build a hidden nest behind the loose bark of conifers. Elsewhere this species is known mostly as a winter resident and a regular, if furtive, part of mixed flocks. Creepers forage by spiraling up the trunks of trees, poking into crevices in the bark to find insects and spiders. When they reach the top, they swoop down to the bottom of the next tree to begin the process again. The bark-covered back offers excellent camouflage, and individuals are most often detected by flashes of movement or the call, a very high, wavering *tseeeee*.

Small and slender, with a thin, curved bill. Cryptic pattern on back and head, white underneath. Long tail.

House Wren

Troglodytes aedon

L 5″ | **WS** 6″

Though visually unassuming, the feisty little House Wren possesses an elaborate rolling, warbling song that makes it a much loved visitor to homes and gardens throughout the Carolinas. In fact, the House Wren is most common in both states near human habitation, where it readily occupies bird houses. This makes for an unusual distribution in the Carolinas, where it is most common in the Piedmont and west in North Carolina and towards the coast in South Carolina, largely following patterns of human density. Most common in the summer months, but many linger through the winter, especially in mild years. Song is a series of bubbly trills on various pitches, typical calls harsh chits and rattles.

Small, light brown all over, palest on throat. Long, thin bill. Longish tail. Black barring on wings and tail.

Winter Wren

Troglodytes hiemalis

L 4″ | **WS** 5.5″

Primarily a bird of northern bogs and spruce forests, the charming, compact Winter Wren nests along the high ridges of the Appalachians as far south as western North Carolina. Elsewhere in the Carolinas it is a widespread but secretive winter resident of wet forests, shrubby tangles, and dense thickets. Like many wrens, it's typically found within three feet of the ground, and when alarmed, will scramble through vegetation or along the ground rather than flying away. Alert and curious; birders can often draw Winter Wrens in by pishing or squeaking, though the birds still prefer to keep some cover between themselves and the observer, calling a punctuated *brrp brp-brp* while flicking the tail and wings. Song, heard mostly in late winter, is a high, long, rambling series of trills.

Small and dark, with a short tail often tipped up. Barred on flanks, wings, and tail.

Sedge Wren

Cistothorus platensis

L 4.5″ | **WS** 5.5″

A secretive resident of coastal marshes, the finely marked
Sedge Wren is an uncommon winter resident along the Coastal
Plain and a rare migrant inland. Sedge Wrens prefer freshwater
and brackish marshes with some shrubs interspersed, or dense
fields and pastures where they can disappear into the grass.
Places like Bodie Lighthouse and Fort Fisher in North Carolina
and Huntington Beach State Park and Bear Island in South
Carolina have traditionally hosted birds between October and
March. Often easier to hear than to see; the typical call is an
abrupt, slightly chirpy *bzzrt*.

Small and straw-colored.
Short tail, often tipped up.
Plain face, unmarked
underparts, bold white
stripes on back. Barred
wings and tail

Marsh Wren

Cistothorus palustris

L 5″ | **WS** 6″

Often little more than a string of gurgling warbles emanating from the cattails, the russet-toned Marsh Wren is a fairly common permanent resident of tidal marshes along the coast of both Carolinas. Despite their ubiquity, these lanky, long-tailed wrens are easily overlooked because of their retiring habits, but they can occasionally be coaxed into view with smacks or squeaks. Reliable at all coastal marshes, they can hardly be missed at Mackay Island and Cedar Island NWRs in North Carolina or in the marshes around Charleston Harbor in South Carolina. Song is a softly mechanical twitter, call a buzzy *frrd frrd* or *chet chet*.

Small and dark, with a long tail, tipped up. Gray breast, rufous upperparts. Dark cap, gray eyebrow. Bold white stripes on back. Barred tail.

Carolina Wren

Thryothorus ludovicianus

L 5.5″ | **WS** 7.5″

The largest and most commonly encountered wren in the Southeast, the cheerful Carolina Wren is a conspicuous permanent resident in all forested or shrubby habitats. Its boisterous and variable three-syllable song, often transcribed as *CHEESEburger CHEESEburger CHEESEburger*, can be heard year-round throughout the Carolinas. A ready adopter of human structures, incorrigibly curious Carolina Wrens are known for wedging their bulky stick nests into any nook or cranny they can find, including but not limited to grills, cable boxes, gutters, eaves, and cinder blocks. In addition to their rollicking songs, they have a number of different calls, including rich *CHEEer* or *Tdip* notes and wheezy *shee shee shee* scolds.

Round and large-headed. Bold white eyebrow and long bill. White cheek and throat. Buffy orange underparts, reddish-brown back, crown, and wings. Faint barring on wings and tail.

Blue-gray Gnatcatcher

Polioptila caerulea

L 4.5″ | **WS** 6″

Slight and long-tailed, the delicate Blue-gray Gnatcatcher is one of the smallest perching birds in the Carolinas. Across most of North and South Carolina, Blue-gray Gnatcatchers are one of the first spring migrants to arrive every year, their thin, wheezy *pzzz pzzzz* calls marking their arrival in mid-March before most trees even begin to leaf out. Increasingly over-winters in the state, primarily on the coast as far north as the Albermarle Peninsula and rarely inland. Blue-gray Gnatcatchers prefer open hardwood forests and shrubby overgrown fields, building a nearly invisible cup nest of spiderweb lined with lichen on a thin horizontal branch. Song is a mismatched series of thin wheezy or scratchy notes.

Small and slender, with a long tail. Short, thin bill. Entirely blue-gray, darker above than below. Tail black from above, white below. Male with short black eyebrow.

Female similar to male, but with plain face lacking eyebrow. Tail paler.

Golden-crowned Kinglet

Regulus satrapa

L 4″ | **WS** 7″

The impish little Golden-crowned Kinglet is a boreal breeder that nests in the high elevation spruce-fir forests of Appalachian North Carolina. Everywhere else in the Carolinas, it is a fairly common winter resident, a familiar part of mixed passerine flocks in the colder months. Distinctive, with a largish head and short tail, Golden-crowned Kinglets feed fairly high in trees, actively flitting around the tips of branches seeking hibernating insects. They're most common in pine or mixed pine-hardwood forests, and are most often detected by their call, a high-pitched whining *tsee-tsee-tsee*.

Very small; short bill and tail. Bold face pattern with yellow crown bordered by black. Black eye stripe. Overall gray-green, darker on back. Yellow edges to flight feathers.

Ruby-crowned Kinglet

Regulus calendula

L 4.25″ | **WS** 7.5″

Cute and impossibly energetic, the Ruby-crowned Kinglet does not breed in the Carolinas, but it's a common migrant and winter resident throughout. Ruby-crowned Kinglets seem to be in constant motion, flitting about the tips of branches seeking insects and flicking their wings and tails during their infrequent pauses. The male's ruby crown is difficult to see unless the bird is worked up, and the most common impression is that of an overall plain bird with a huge eye and tiny bill. Song is like a pull-toy, a build-up of thin whistles followed by an explosion of whistled trills. Calls include annoyed *chits*.

Very small; short bill and tail. Plain face with large dark eye, white eye ring. Gray-brown body, yellow edges on flight feathers.

Blue Ridge Birding

The Blue Ridge Mountains of the western Carolinas are biological islands, relics of ecosystems forced south during the last ice age and left high and dry when the glaciers receded. At the highest elevations, the spruce-fir zone harbors many species of birds, as well as a great many other plants and animals, that are more typically found in the northern US and Canada, while the lower valleys and surrounding lowlands offer typical species of the Southeast. The difference is so stark that a short drive from the Piedmont foothills to the top of Mount Mitchell offers as much ecological diversity as traveling from Columbia, South Carolina, to the Adirondacks of New York!

Birding the region is made easier by paying attention to changes in elevation and the changing flora at different altitudes. Lowland hardwood forests become increasingly interspersed with conifers as you climb, eventually becoming entirely coniferous around 5,000 feet. Attention to the plants around you can be the difference between determining whether you are seeing Alder (higher elevation) or Willow (lower elevation) Flycatchers, or hearing Blue-headed (higher elevation) and Red-eyed (lower elevation) Vireos, among others.

The spazzy burbling song of Winter Wren is a common summer sound in the higher elevations of the Blue Ridge Mountains.

Eastern Bluebird

Sialia sialis

L 7″ | **WS** 13″

A friendly, bull-necked Eastern Bluebird perched on a power line or barbed wire fence is a familiar sight year-round in the rural open country of the Carolinas. After decades of decline in the middle of last century, a concerted effort was made to encourage the installation of nest boxes throughout the eastern US. The species responded spectacularly, and the tall, rectangular houses in pastures and open areas are as common in parts of the Piedmont as the bird are themselves. Mostly loners during the warmer months, bluebirds band together in nomadic flocks in the winter, often with robins and waxwings, seeking fruited trees. Birds in flight seem comma-shaped, and give a lazy little *CHEE-o-up call*. The song is a series of breezy melodious phrases.

Medium-sized, full-chested and short-tailed. Large round head. Male has bright blue back, wings, and head. Orangey breast, throat, and flanks. White belly. Bill small and dark.

Female similar to male, but dingier on head, breast, and back. Blue wings and tail.

Young birds in summer with scaly breast, speckled back. Blue wings and tail.

Veery
Catharus fuscescens

L 7" | **WS** 12"

Elegantly attired in soft, rich reddish browns, the reclusive Veery breeds along the spine of the Appalachians into North Carolina. In the rest of the Carolinas, it's an uncommon migrant in both spring and fall, a nice find in moist forests with plenty of understory cover. Like many other migrant thrushes, it is attracted to fruiting trees in fall, and dogwood berries are a particular favorite. Best known for its elaborate and ethereal song, heard regularly in spring and summer in places like Mount Mitchell State Park and Pisgah National Forest, a descending series of swirling notes more like a laser gun in a sci-fi movie than a bird. Call a discordant *vzeer*.

Medium-sized, with small head and long legs. Rich reddish brown on head, back, and tail. Eye ring indistinct or absent. Spots restricted to upper breast fairly faint and occasional only a brownish wash.

Gray-cheeked Thrush
Catharus minimus

L 7.25″ | **WS** 13″

Less common in the Carolinas than the very similar Swainson's Thrush, and with a colder gray-brown look, the Gray-cheeked Thrush is an uncommon migrant in both states, mostly in the western half of the Carolinas. It is a relatively late spring migrant, and is easy to miss in that season, as it comes and goes almost entirely in the first two weeks of May. More reliable in fall, from September through late October; many state parks in the Piedmont and west offer the well-forested areas where thrushes prefer to stop over. Like most thrushes, they love fruiting trees, so staking out a dogwood or hackberry in the fall might produce Gray-cheeked and other thrushes. Doesn't often sing in the Carolinas, but call note is a squirty *chee-ip*.

Medium-sized, cold gray-brown back. Breast with dense dark spots. Eye ring indistinct or absent. Face grayish behind eye.

Swainson's Thrush

Catharus ustulatus

L 7" | **WS** 12"

More numerous and more richly colored than the similar Gray-cheeked Thrush, Swainson's Thrush is a fairly common migrant across the whole of the Carolinas, and almost certainly a breeding bird in the higher mountains of western North Carolina. Passes through the Carolinas from mid-April through May and again in September and October. Swainson's Thrushes prefer well-forested areas with fairly dense undergrowth, as found in many Piedmont and western region state parks. Like many thrushes, they are attracted to fruiting trees in the fall. Song is a series of ascending gossamer swirls, call a liquid *bwit*.

Medium-sized; warm brown back and head. Bold buffy eye ring, buffy wash on face and chin. Spotting on breast warm brown, moderately dense

Hermit Thrush

Catharus guttatus

L .6.75″ | **WS** 11.5″

The jaunty Hermit Thrush is the only spotted thrush to regularly winter in the Carolinas. From October through April it's a fairly common, if reclusive, denizen of shrubby thickets, forests with dense understory, and hedgerows. Like most thrushes, it is attracted to fruiting trees, and winter-fruiting shrubs like American holly and beautyberry are important food sources. Hermit Thrushes are scattered breeders above 5,000 feet in elevation in western North Carolina, and can be found in spruce-fir forests on the higher mountains such as Mount Mitchell and Roan Mountain. Song is similar to other spotted thrushes, but begins with a high, clear single note, followed by airy swirls. Common calls include a percolating *chup chup* and a whiney *zheeee*.

Medium-sized; warm brown back and head. Breast with dense dark spots. Reddish tail and rump much brighter than back. White eye ring obvious.

Wood Thrush

Hylocichla mustelina

L 8″ | **WS** 13″

Few species have seen their population decline in recent decades as much as the pot-bellied, golden-voiced Wood Thrush. Still fairly common in shady hardwood forests throughout the Carolinas, the species seems to be harder to find with every passing year. More often heard than seen, the thrush's slurred, echoing *EEE-o-LAEY-breeee* rings out from the dense under-story of mature woods, the singer rarely more than 15 feet above the ground. Most reliable at many of the state parks in the Piedmont and mountains in both states, mostly in places where unbroken woodlands have been protected. Arrives in April and mostly departs by mid-October. Often calls an annoyed *bwet bwet bwet* when disturbed.

Larger than other thrushes, with extensive bold spots on chin, breast, and flanks. Bright white eye ring. Warm brown above, brightest on neck and head. Large bill.

The deeper "pot-belly" and thick bill of Wood Thrush give it a much different silhouette than other migratory thrushes.

American Robin

Turdus migratorius

L 10″ | **WS** 14″

A familiar symbol of suburbia continent-wide, the handsome, portly American Robin might better be named the "lawn thrush." A permanent resident in the Carolinas, robins spend their summers defending territories in semi-open habitats like lawns and parks, where they scamper across the grass, pausing frequently and cocking the head in search of invertebrates hidden just below the surface. In the winter, they gather in nomadic flocks traveling widely in search of food, often in the company of waxwings and bluebirds. These often very large flocks descend en masse to devour berries or seeds from fruiting trees before moving on. The pleasant, slurred song is a common part of the suburban soundscape, a series of two- and three-note phrases often written as *cheer-up cheerily cheer-o*. Gives many calls, including a hearty chuckle, a high *tseeee,* and a *cheee-pup* in flight.

Fairly large, with round body, smallish head. Males brightly colored with brick-red breast, black head with white eye arcs, bright yellow bill. In flight, small white corners on tail.

Female patterned like male, but generally more washed out.

Young birds in summer and fall messy-looking, with speckled breast and back. Indistinct markings on face, darker bill.

Gray Catbird
Dumetella carolinensis

L 8.5″ | **WS** 11″

Sleek and shy, the slate-colored Gray Catbird is a common summer resident across the whole of the Carolinas, and retreats to the coast in the winter. Catbirds prefer dense tangles, where they skulk patiently through the brush, dragging their long tail behind them listlessly. They can be found anywhere with heavy brush, hedgerows, or overgrown fields. They're rather common in suburban landscapes, but would be easily overlooked if not for their eponymous call, a whiney *meeERRR,* not unlike an annoyed cat. Song is a disjointed series of short squeaky whistles, interspersed with *chat* calls and whines.

Medium-sized, with long tail. Entirely slate gray, with a large dark eye and black cap. Brick-red undertail not often seen.

Brown Thrasher

Toxostoma rufum

L 12″ | **WS** 13″

Flashy, with a long reddish tail and piercing yellow eye, the
Brown Thrasher is the largest of the three "mimic thrushes"
found in the Carolinas. Thrashers get their name from their
habit of tossing aside leaf litter as they forage for invertebrates
and fruit close to the ground. Present year-round across both
states, they can be conspicuous in the summer months, singing
loudly from exposed perches in brushy fields and hedgerows, and are often fairly common in suburban landscapes
with enough cover. In the winter, however, they turn into real
skulkers, creeping through dense cover close to the ground as
inconspicuously as possible. Song is a varied combination of
slurred whistles and harsher notes, always paired, and often
incorporating elements of other species' songs. Calls are a
variety of *smacks* and *churrs*.

Fairly large, with a long tail
and a long curved bill. Rich
rufous upperparts, nape,
and crown. Dense dark
streaks on breast becoming
thinner towards the belly.
Bright yellow eye on pale
face. Two thin wing bars.

Northern Mockingbird
Mimus polyglottos

L 10″ | **WS** 14″

The species name of the garrulous Northern Mockingbird, *polyglottos*, means "many-tongued," and there is hardly a more appropriate descriptor for this audacious songbird. Common across the Carolinas in open and semi-open habitats, mockingbirds are easily found in the summer months in parks, neighborhoods, farms, and brushy fields, typically sitting atop a small tree, post, or wire singing a rambling song that incorporates imitations of many sounds in the bird's vicinity, including but not limited to other birds, squirrels, and car alarms. Individual sounds are often doubled or tripled. Mockingbirds are generally extremely territorial when defending a nest or a food source, chasing away any perceived threat, whether bird, mammal, or other. Calls include a hoarse *wreeeh* and a harsh *chewt*.

Medium-sized and lanky. Pale gray all over, darker on wings and tail. Thin eye stripe. White patches in wings. In flight, shows distinctive flashy white patches in wings and tail.

European Starling

Sturnus vulgaris

L 8.5″ | **WS** 14″

Often considered a nuisance despite its shimmering attractive appearance, the non-native European Starling is a common to abundant permanent resident in cities, towns, and agricultural regions. Starlings are quite gregarious, often found in flocks of a dozen or more. In winter, they join mixed flocks of blackbirds and cowbirds that can number into the hundreds of thousands. Their short tail and pot-bellied shape differentiate them from blackbirds, and along with their pointed wings, makes them look like little triangles in flight. Skilled mimics, they can imitate the vocalizations of a number of bird species, particularly those with whistled songs, such as bobwhites and pewees. Song is a series of hisses and chatters.

Medium-sized and stocky, with short tail and large head and bill. Breeding adult (left) glossy purple-black. Bright yellow bill and pink legs. Nonbreeding adult (below) dark with extensive pale spots. Bill dark early in the winter, becoming paler as the season wears on.

American Pipit

Anthus rubescens

L 6.5" | **WS** 10.5"

Despite being a quite common winter resident, the slender American Pipit is incredibly easy to overlook. Pipits are birds of open country, preferring plowed fields, overgrazed pastures, exposed mudflats, and closely sheared lawns, where entire flocks can disappear into the background. With longish legs, American Pipit walks across the ground in fits and starts, constantly bobbing its tail, and is typically invisible until the flocks flush. Once birders learn the flight call, a bouncy *tsi-pit tsi-pi-tit*, they begin to find pipits passing overhead in many places on the Coastal Plain and in the Piedmont from October through April.

Small and thin, with a longish tail and short, thin bill. Long legs. Mostly plain brown upperparts, with dense streaks on breast and flanks. Paler eyebrow, plain chin. In flight, tail is dark with bright white outer feathers.

Cedar Waxwing

Bombycilla cedrorum

L 7" | **WS** 12"

Like a figure from an oil painting, the elegant, crested Cedar
Waxwing is a permanent resident in the mountains of western
North Carolina and a common but erratic winter resident
elsewhere. Almost always found in groups, flocks of a dozen to
a hundred wander throughout the Carolinas in winter in search
of fruiting trees, a significant part of their diet year-round.
Waxwings can be identified in flight by their whirring wingbeats
and compact flocks; birds flying overhead are constantly calling,
a cacophony of high-pitched, slightly trilled *seeeeeee* calls.

Fairly small and compact, with
bold black mask and obvious crest.
Mostly tan, with pale yellow belly.
Bright yellow band at tip of tail.

Ovenbird

Seiurus aurocapilla

L 6″ | **WS** 9.5″

Pot-bellied and skulky, the subtle Ovenbird resembles a thrush more than a warbler. A fairly common summer resident throughout the Carolinas in forests with sparse broad-leaf undergrowth, the Ovenbird is named for the unique covered "oven-like" nest it hides in the leafy cover of the forest floor. Ovenbirds spend most of their time close to the ground, walking rather than hopping though the woods, as they searches for invertebrates in the leaf litter. Males arrive in late March and immediately beginning singing from the forest midstory, rarely more than 20 feet off the ground. Typical song is a rolling *cherty cherty CHERTY CHERTY CHERTY*, increasing in volume and stridency. Most are gone by the end of October, but a few linger through the winter in dense coastal forests.

Large for a warbler, short-tailed. Greenish-brown back and wings, densely spotted white breast. White eye ring, two black stripes on crown.

Worm-eating Warbler

Helmitheros vermivorum

L 5.25″ | **WS** 8.5″

Large-billed, short-tailed, and in all aspects rather strange, the Worm-eating Warbler is an uncommon breeding bird in various scattered parts of the Carolinas. Most common in the lower mountains of the west, where it breeds in rhododendron and mountain laurel groves, often on steep terrain. Along the Coastal Plain south to Horry County, South Carolina, it prefers swamp thickets around bay lakes. Migrants can be found anywhere. In all habitats, the Worm-eating Warbler is known for its unique method of foraging, in which it probes dead leaves on the tips of branches for insect larvae. Arrives in April and present through October; song is a buzzy trill, easily mistaken for an insect.

Compact, with a short tail and a large, flat head. Bill large. Olive on back and wings, buffy tan elsewhere. Striped head distinctive.

Black-and-white Warbler

Mniotilta varia

L 5.25″ | **WS** 8.25″

This unique little warbler behaves like a nuthatch, creeping
carefully up and down the trunks and branches of trees in
search of insects hiding in the bark. The zebra-striped Black-
and-White Warbler is found year-round in the Carolinas. It is a
breeding bird across both states, mostly in the mountains, and a
common spring and fall migrant and uncommon wintering bird
along the coast, especially in southern South Carolina. While
they show no particular preference for any forest type, Black-
and-white Warblers can be found readily in the hardwood and
mixed forests of the west in spring and fall. Song is a high
and thin *weeseeweeseeweeseeweesee*, sometimes likened to a
squeaky wheel.

Bold black and white stripes
all over. Male with black face
and throat. White eye ring.
Female and fall and winter
birds similar. Face plain.
Black and white stripes on
back and wings.

Louisiana Waterthrush

Parkesia motacilla

L 6" | **WS** 10"

One of the first migrants to arrive in spring, the streaky, clear-voiced Louisiana Waterthrush is closely associated with rocky streams and rivers throughout the Carolinas. Starting in late February, you can find these large warblers spaced regularly along the banks of waterways that flow through hardwood forests. Foraging birds constantly bob tail. Song is loud, consisting of three sweet slurred whistles followed by a jumbled series of notes that carries above the sound of rushing water. Also an early migrant in the fall, Louisiana Waterthrushes disappear abruptly by the end of August. Call note is a loud *SMACK*.

Large for a warbler; long-bodied, with a large, flat head. Heavy bill. Brown back and wings, white underparts with sparse broad streaks. Bold white eyebrow equally thick throughout. Legs usually pinkish. Chin plain.

Northern Waterthrush

Parkesia noveboracensis

L 6″ | **WS** 9.5″

Darker and streakier than the Louisiana Waterthrush, the
Northern Waterthrush is only a transient in the Carolinas,
passing through both states briefly from mid-April through
mid-May and again from August through October. More
commonly associated with standing water than the Louisiana,
Northern Waterthrushes prowl the banks of boggy seeps and
well-vegetated ponds, bobbing their entire back end constantly
as they seek out invertebrates. Song is an accelerating series of
liquid slurred notes. Call is a cold *SPINCK*.

Large for a warbler; brown
above, dingy yellowish
below. Streaks on breast
shorter than in Louisiana
and quite dense. Bill smalle
thinner. Legs usually
brownish. Eyebrow yellowis
narrower behind the eye.

Golden-winged Warbler

Vermivora chrysoptera

L 4.75" | **WS** 7.5"

Highly local as a breeder and fairly rare as a migrant, the gaudy Golden-winged Warbler is sadly declining across much of its range, including the Carolinas. A few still breed in North Carolina's mountains between 3,000 and 4,000 feet in elevation, in transitory habitats such as overgrown fields, powerline cuts, and shrubby bogs. Max Patch Road in Haywood County and Stecoah Gap in Graham County have regularly hosted breeding birds. They're often under threat from more generalist species like Chestnut-sided and Blue-winged Warblers, and readily interbreed with the latter. Migrants can be found anywhere, typically with other migrating warblers, but are quite rare. Song a buzzy *ZEEEE-zuh-zuh-zuh-zuh*.

Short-tailed, with small thin bill. Male with bold face pattern, black mask and throat, bright yellow forehead and crown. Gray body, large yellow wing patch.

Female similar to male, but face pattern more washed out.

Blue-winged Warbler

Vermivora cyanoptera

L 4.75″ | **WS** 7.5″

Striking in appearance, with a black eye line and neat white wing bars, Blue-winged Warblers are uncommon migrants throughout the Carolinas and a likely but still unconfirmed breeder in western North Carolina. Blue-winged Warblers prefer brushy habitats, overgrown pastures with medium-sized trees and woodland edges with lots of weeds and tangles. Passes through the Carolinas in late April and early May and again in September. Most common in the west, rarer towards the coast. Song is a groaning *beee-BRRRRRRZZZ.*

Bright yellow with blue-gray wings. Male brighter, with two white wing bars. Black eye stripe. Yellow belly, white undertail. Spring and fall plumages identical.

Female similar to male but duller, with more olive head, thinner wing bars.

Prothonotary Warbler
Protonotaria citrea

L 5.5" | **WS** 8.75"

A glowing ball of sunlight in the dark swamps, the Prothonotary Warbler is a classic bird of southeastern bottomland forests. Stocky and short-tailed, they typically arrive in the Carolinas in April and are most common along the Coastal Plain, less so towards the mountains. Hard to miss between April and September at places like Alligator River NWR and Croatan National Forest in NC or Santee NWR and Francis Marion National Forest in SC. Almost always found near water, the Prothonotary Warbler is one of the few species of cavity-nesting warblers in North America and will use small next boxes placed above shady still water. Song is an emphatic ringing *sweet sweet SWEET SWEET SWEET*, increasing in volume.

Short-tailed, with large head. Male with entirely golden yellow head, breast, and belly. Eye large and dark. Bill heavy and black. Wings blue-gray. Back olive.

Female more olive on head, less bright overall. Eye large on plain face. Large black bill. Whitish on belly.

Swainson's Warbler

Limnothlypis swainsonii

L 5.5" | **WS** 9"

Plain and dumpy in appearance, but with a clear, ringing voice, Swainson's Warbler is one of the most sought-after warblers in the Southeast. The short-tailed, heavy-billed skulker can be found in two different habitats in the Carolinas. On the Coastal Plain, it prefers impenetrable stands of giant cane wherever it grows, while in the southern mountains it is closely associated with dense rhododendron groves, often on rocky terrain near river and streams. Present in the Carolinas from mid-April through September, they're easiest find in spring and early summer, when their rich, slurred song rings out from tangled vegetation, rendered as *Eew Eew I-stepped-in Poo*. Easy to hear, not always easy to see, at Howell Woods and Croatan National Forest in North Carolina, Congeree National Park and Edisto Nature Trail in South Carolina.

Short-tailed, deep-bellied, with a large flat head and large bill. Rusty cap, beige eyebrow, black eye stripe. Unstreaked tan underparts. Plain brown back and wings.

Tennessee Warbler

Oreothlypis peregrina

L 4.75" | **WS** 7.75"

Dainty and short-tailed, with a thin, sharp bill, Tennessee Warbler occurs in the Carolinas only in migration. Uncommon in spring, mostly in the first week of May, the more leisurely southward trip takes them through the Appalachians, where they are easily the most common migrating warbler in September and early October. Hard to miss in fall along the Blue Ridge Parkway in North Carolina or around Caesar's Head and Sassafras Mountain in South Carolina. Generally sticks to the upper story of the forest, but will come lower in fall when mixed in flocks of other migrants. Song, infrequently head in the Carolinas, is an accelerating three-part trill *chipchipchip-chip tsweetsweetsweetswee pititititit*.

Small and short-tailed. Green back and wings, gray head with white eyebrow, black eye stripe. White underneath, notably under the tail.

Fall birds uniformly yellow-green. Sometimes very similar to Orange-crowned Warbler. White undertail contrasts with belly. Pale eyebrow, dark eye stripe.

Orange-crowned Warbler

Oreothlypis celeta

L 5" | **WS** 7.25"

An uncommon wintering bird near the coast and a fairly rare migrant elsewhere, the poorly named Orange-crowned Warbler is easy to overlook. The eponymous orange crown is little more than a sliver of feathers atop the head and almost never seen. More diagnostic is the overall plain green plumage and the small, sharp bill. Similar in some plumages to the Tennessee Warbler, Orange-crowns arrive in the Carolinas much later in the fall, at earliest in mid-October, and leave by the end of April. They prefer shrubby tangles and wooded thickets in winter, at places like Mattamuskeet NWR and Fort Fisher in North Carolina, and throughout the Lower Coastal Plain in South Carolina. Does not usually sing in the Carolinas, but call is a tinny *snick*.

Small, sharp-billed. Uniformly greenish or green-gray. White or yellowish eye arcs. Always yellowish undertail.

Nashville Warbler
Oreothlypis ruficapilla

L 4.75" | **WS** 7.5"

Most Nashville Warblers migrate west of the Appalachians, and this the species is an uncommon migrant in the Carolinas. They can be found just about anywhere in both spring and fall, but they are most reliably seen in the mountains from late August through mid-October. Generally prefers forest canopies, but often descends to scrubby thickets and weedy fields in fall where it can be confused with Palm or Orange-crowned Warbler. Fairly rare on the coast, but regular, with individuals occasionally lingering well into winter. Doesn't often sing in the Carolinas, but call note is a high *tsiip*.

mall; short tail. Gray head, green
ack. Bold white eye ring. Yellow
hroat and breast. Alternating pattern
f yellow (breast), white (belly), and
ellow (undertail) distinctive. Female
imilar but more washed out.

Wilson's Warbler

Cardellina pusilla

L 4.75″ | **WS** 7″

A cute yellow warbler with a distinctive black skullcap, the Wilson's Warbler is only an uncommon migrant in the Carolinas, despite its incredibly broad breeding range across the north of the entire continent. Equally uncommon in both spring and fall, and in all corners of the states, finding a Wilson's Warbler requires a bit of luck, and a close scrutiny of the wet shrubby habitats and woodland edges where they can be found in May, and again from late August through October. Some birds linger into winter, and there are a handful of records throughout the Coastal Plan and Piedmont into January. Song is simple and variable, a series of short, slurry accelerating notes *tsweets-weetsweetsweetswee*, and call is a chirpy *jint*.

Round body, long tail, large head with large dark eye on plain face. Entirely yellow, greener on back. Male with small black cap. Female less bright, without well-defined cap.

Canada Warbler

Cardellina canadensis

L 5.25″ | **WS** 8″

Stylish in broad strokes of gray and yellow, the energetic
Canada Warbler is a common breeding bird in the mountain
west and an uncommon migrant elsewhere. Closely associated
with rhododendron groves, this long-tailed warbler is inquisi-
tive, often creeping close in response to squeaking or pishing,
swishing its tail back and forth. Fairly common above 3,000
feet along the Blue Ridge Parkway and in far northwest South
Carolina from late April through September. Can be found
anywhere in migration, generally preferring shrubby habitats
and wooded edges. Song is a jumble of squeaky notes, *ta-wish-
ity-t-wishity-t-woo*; call a dry *shpit*.

Long-tailed, plain gray
above including tail.
Yellow underneath.
Male with bold black
necklace across breast.
Bold eye ring on black
and yellow face.

Female similar to male, but
with patterns less distinct.

Kentucky Warbler

Geothlypis formosa

L 5.25″ | **WS** 8.5″

A relatively large warbler with flashy Elvis Presley sideburns, Kentucky Warbler is a fairly common breeding bird in extensive hardwood forests with dense undergrowth. Stays close to the ground, walking or slinking through low vegetation. Most common in the mountain west, though only at lower elevations, and fairly uncommon and local elsewhere, Kentucky Warblers are easiest to find in from mid-April through early summer, when males sing vociferously from the mid-story, a rich burry *prCHRR prCHRR prCHRR prCHRR,* similar to Carolina Wren but less clearly enunciated. Can be found along the Blue Ridge Parkway below 2,500 feet, but most easily encountered at sites in the Coastal Plain like Howell Woods in North Carolina and Edisto Nature Trail in South Carolina.

Short-tailed and pudgy. Entirely yellow underparts. Male with bold black "sideburns," yellow eyebrow wrapping around eye, black forecrown. Olive green back, wings, tail. Female similar, with less distinct face pattern.

Common Yellowthroat

Geothlypis trichas

L 5″ | **WS** 6.75″

Bold and curious, the Common Yellowthroat is one of the most common warblers throughout the Carolinas year-round. They prefer scrubby habitats, preferably around water, and are at home in fresh and salt marshes, overgrown fields, wet pastures, and woodland edges. Less common in winter, most retreating towards the coast or south of the Carolinas. Stays low and hidden in brush most of the time, flicking from thicket to thicket, but can be easy to rile up with pishing or squeaking. Sings frequently, a rhythmic *t-witchit-t-witchit-t-witchit*. Call is a brusque *chttt*.

Male with black bandito mask bordered by white. Green-brown body; bright yellow throat, breast, and undertail.

Female plain, with large dark eye. Greenish body, yellow throat and breast. Young males similar, but often show incomplete, messy mask.

Hooded Warbler

Setophaga citrina

L 5.25" | **WS** 7"

Few warblers are as arresting as a well-seen male Hooded Warbler. The stunning little sprite is a fairly common breeding bird in hardwood forests with dense understory across the entirety of the Carolinas. Typically stays well below the canopy, rarely above 20 feet or so, where it flicks about in dark corners flashing the white patches in its long tail. Can be found at many protected areas with intact forest, including state parks and national forests in both states. Present from April well into October, but easiest to find in spring and summer, when males are singing, a sweet slurred song that can be transcribed as *the red the red TEE-shirt*. Call is a modest *tsink*.

Male unmistakable. Yellow face surrounded by black hood. Green back, entirely yellow underparts. Obvious white flashes in tail.

Female similar to male, but hood less extensive, entirely absent in youngest birds.

Cerulean Warbler

Setophaga cerulea

L 4.75″ | **WS** 7.75″

The delicate, Carolina-blue Cerulean Warbler is one of the most rapidly declining songbirds in North America. It's an uncommon and highly local breeder in the mountains of North Carolina, and formerly bred in South Carolina and on the northeastern Coastal Plain. Prefers montane hardwood forests, typically on steep slopes below 3,500 feet. Cerulean Warblers nest in loose colonies, so where one male is singing there are usually one or two more nearby. It spends most of its time high in the treetops, so getting a good look at the glowing blue back is difficult. The best spot to find them is on the Blue Ridge Parkway, northeast of Asheville, North Carolina, between Craven Gap and Craggy Gardens. Drive slowly and listen for the buzzy song, *zhrr zhrr zhrr zhrr zippity zeeeee.*

Small; male with sky blue upper parts. Mostly bright white below, with dark breastband and streaks on flanks. Two white wing bars.

Female with aquamarine upperparts, plain face with large dark eye. Grayish streaks on flanks. Pale eyebrow.

American Redstart

Setophaga ruticilla

L 5.25″ | **WS** 7.75″

An active little warbler clad in Halloween colors, the American Redstart is a common breeding bird at scattered sites across both states and a very common migrant in both spring and fall. Breeds in hardwood forests in the mountains and north-eastern Coastal Plain, but in migration can be found just about anywhere with brushy cover. Redstarts are active and erratic as they feed, flitting back and forth with tail fanned and wings slightly drooped, dropping between thin branches like a falling leaf. Song, a high *tswee tswee tswee tsweedibop tswee*, is variable and can resemble the songs of several other warbler species. Call is a squeaky *chip*.

Thin, with a long tail. Males unmistakable, black with orange patches on wings, tail, and breast sides. White belly.

Females and young birds patterned like adult male, but gray-green body and yellow patches on wings, tail, and breast sides.

Males take two years to attain adult plumage. Young males in their first summer often with black spots on head and body.

Cape May Warbler

Setophaga tigrina

L 5″ | **WS** 8.25″

A breeding bird in the boreal forests across northern Canada, the tiger-striped Cape May Warbler is only a brief visitor to the Carolinas in spring and fall. More common in the interior than on the coast, on its northward journey it is an uncommon migrant, mostly through the western third. When it comes back through in September and October, it can be found more commonly throughout. Often found in the forest canopy, hardwood or mixed, in spring, seems to prefer pine trees in the Piedmont and Coastal Plain on its southbound return. A few birds linger into winter, and can turn up at feeding stations in the Piedmont and Coastal Plain. Song is a high, thin *seep-seep-seep-seep*.

Small, with pointy bill. Male has yellow breast with extensive dark streaking. Yellow wraps around neck. Rufous around ears, dark cap. White wing patch.

Females and fall birds similar. Heavy black streaks on pale yellow breast. Pale on sides of neck and ear.

Young females can be extremely plain, with very limited streaking. Pale spot around ear present in all plumages. Small bill.

Northern Parula

Setophaga americana

L 4.5″ | **WS** 7″

An energetic ball of blue and yellow, the Northern Parula is one of the more common warblers throughout the Carolinas. An early migrant, parulas begin to make their presence known in late March. Males sing a buzzy, rising *zzzzzzzzzzzzzz-UP!* or a misfiring *zzipita zzipita zup zup zup ZUP*, like a tiny motor revving, that is hard to miss in spring. Most common in bottomland forests on the Coastal Plain, parulas prefer to nest in places where they can find Spanish moss or beard lichen in which they can hide their nests. In the Piedmont and west, they are fairly common in hardwood forests, generally near water. One of the most common migrating warblers in fall, they can be found in mixed flocks of migrants through October.

Breeding male (above) with blue-gray head, bright white eye arcs. Yellow throat and upper breast separated by black and orange breast band. Olive back, two bold wing bars. Bill dark above, yellow beneath. Female (left) and fall birds similar. Like breeding male but washed out. Breast band weak or absent. Eye arcs smaller.

Magnolia Warbler

Setophaga magnolia

L 5″ | **WS** 7.5″

Lanky, with flashy white flags in the tail, the Magnolia Warbler
is a fairly common migrant in the Carolinas, particularly
in fall. Most common in the western third, Magnolias have
infrequently nested in the high mountains of North Carolina.
Spring migrants stay more to the west, but in fall the species
is one of the more common migrants throughout, even on the
coast. They generally stay in the mid-story, preferring brushy
areas, second-growth forests, and willow groves. Typical song is
simple and short, a squeaky *WIDer WIDer WIDey-est*. Call is a
high, weak, *tsit*.

Breeding male striking, with
bold black mask, yellow
breast with coarse black
stripes. White eyebrow.
Large white wing patch.
Blue-gray crown, dark back.
Undertail pattern, with
broad black tip, distinctive
in all plumages.

Females and nonbreeding
birds similar. Gray head,
yellow throat and breast
with limited or absent
streaking. Two thin white
wing bars. White eye ring.
Tail with wide black tip.

Bay-breasted Warbler

Setophaga castanea

L 5.5" | **WS** 9"

An attractive, richly-plumaged warbler of the northern boreal forests, Bay-breasted Warblers are only transient in the Carolinas. Their spring migration route mostly takes them west of the Appalachians, and as such they are an uncommon to rare migrant in early May, primarily in the far west. In fall, though, they are a common and occasionally very common migrant, particularly in the western half of the states. Unfortunately, by that point the males have molted out of their russet plumage and can be easily confused with Blackpoll or Pine Warblers. Fairly reliable in September and October along the Blue Ridge Parkway, or in the northwest mountains of South Carolina.

Breeding male with black mask and chestnut cap, throat, and flanks. Pale belly. Crisp white wing bars, striped back.

Female and fall birds similar. Mostly plain head. Buffy, sometimes rufous, flank; crisp wing bars.

Blackburnian Warbler

Setophaga fusca

L 5″ | **WS** 8.5″

Easily one of the most spectacular birds in North America, the flame-throated Blackburnian Warbler is a boreal nesting bird that breeds south along the spine of the Appalachian Mountains into the Carolinas. A fairly common breeding bird above 4,500 feet, elsewhere it is an uncommon migrant, mostly in the Piedmont and Mountains, and rare in the east. Blackburnian Warblers arrive in late April, and males can be quite conspicuous along the Blue Ridge Parkway or at Sassafras Mountain in SC before the trees leaf out. They sing a rising three-part song, *ter ter ter ter tipitipitipitipi tseeeeeeeee*, the last note reaching a very high frequency. In migration, can be found in any forest habitat, but tend to stay in the canopy, where they can be easily missed.

Breeding male unmistakable, with bright orange throat and breast. Black and orange face with dark cheek. Black streaking on flanks. Dark back, large white wing patch.

Female and nonbreeding birds with similar pattern, but washed out. Yellow-orange throat, dark cheek. Gray back.

Yellow Warbler

Setophaga petechia

L 5″ | **WS** 8″

Of the many species of warbler in North America, this species is the only one that is entirely yellow. The cheery, cute Yellow Warbler is a bird closely associated with wetland thickets and willow groves, and is fairly common in such habitats in the western half of the Carolinas. Elsewhere it is known primarily as a migrant and a scattered and declining breeder. Spring birds arrive in mid-April, singing a rhythmic *sweet sweet sweet tititoto sweet*. Call is a loud, rich *tship*. Leaves the Carolinas by the end of October.

Breeding male entirely bright yellow. Large dark eye on plain face. Narrow reddish-brown streaks on breast and along flanks.

Females and nonbreeding birds entirely yellow-green or dull yellow. Plain face with large dark eye.

Chestnut-sided Warbler

Setophaga pensylvanica

L 5″ | **WS** 7.75″

The term "confusing fall warbler" probably applies best to the stout Chestnut-sided Warbler, whose striking breeding plumage is replaced by an almost unrecognizable gray-green in the fall. They're common to very common breeding birds in the Appalachians to northwest South Carolina and uncommon migrants in the Piedmont, mostly in fall, fairly rare on the coast. The Chestnut-sided Warbler stays relatively low, flitting about with its tail cocked at a jaunty angle. Prefers second-growth forest and brushy edges, and will aggressively defend its territory, a behavior that has been suggested to contribute to the decline of the Golden-winged Warbler in the Carolinas. Song is an emphatic *swee swee swee swee SWEEswitchEW*. Call a chirpy *chipt*.

Breeding male with very white underparts, bright yellow crown, white cheeks. Black moustache extends to coarse chestnut streak across flanks. Yellow-green streaks on back, tail often cocked.

Females and nonbreeding birds very different. Gray face and underparts. Bright green cap and back. Bold white eye ring. Crisp yellow wing bars. Often with chestnut streaks on flanks.

Blackpoll Warbler

Setophaga striata

L 5.5″ | **WS** 9″

The arrival of migrating Blackpoll Warblers in mid-May is usually a sign to Carolina birders that the trickle of north-bound migrants is about to stop. A fairly common transient throughout both states, the species takes different routes in each season. In the spring, the skunk-headed version of the bird travels up the middle of the continent, passing mostly through the mountains and the Piedmont. In the fall, clad in subtle streaks, most travel down the coast to about Cape Hatteras, where they take off over the ocean on one long flight to South America. Migrants are less common inland. Found in most woodland habitats, staying towards the tops of trees, males are revealed by their high pitched song, *tsi tsi tsi tsi TSITSITSITSI tsi tsi tsi,* like the failing brakes on an old car.

Breeding male striking, with chickadee-like face pattern, black cap and white cheek. Bright white underneath with fine streaks along flank. Gray back, bright orange legs and feet.

Breeding females finely streaked on face, back and flanks. Mostly pale underneath. Yellowish legs.

In fall, Blackpolls become greenish-yellow all over. Two bright wing bars. Note faint streaking on breast and flanks, orange feet on black legs. Compare with unstreaked underparts of fall Bay-breasted Warbler.

Black-throated Blue Warbler

Setophaga caerulescens

L 5.25" | **WS** 7.75"

Handsome in bold blocks of color, the Black-throated Blue
Warbler is one of the more common migrant warblers in the
Carolinas in both spring and fall. This understory-loving
warbler is also a breeding bird in the mountains above 2,500
feet, and fairly easy to find there from mid-April through
October. Hard to miss along the Blue Ridge Parkway, breeding
well into South Carolina on higher mountains like Caesar's
Head and Sassafras Mountain. Regular song a buzzy sighing
zho zhey zheeeee, sometimes transcribed as *so lay-zeeee*. Call is
a simple dry *tzik*, like a junco.

Male boldly tri-colored.
Black mask and throat
surrounded by blue-gray
crown and back, bright
white breast and belly.
Small white patch in wing.

Female fairly plain.
Brownish overall, darker
above than below. Face
darker, bordered by white
eyebrow. Often with a small
white patch in the wing.

Palm Warbler

Setophaga palmorum

L 5.5″ | **WS** 8″

This ground-loving warbler might better be called "wagtail warbler" for its habit of constantly bopping its tail as it strolls along the ground. The Palm Warbler is a common migrant and wintering bird along the coast and in most of lowland South Carolina. Two distinct subspecies pass through the Carolinas every year. One, bright yellow underneath, nests in eastern Canada, and the other, streakier with a white belly, nests in the boreal forests of west-central Canada. The latter is more common and the more likely subspecies to spend the winter. Song is a buzzy twitter about 2 seconds long, *zrizrizrizrizrizrizri*, call a chirpy *shidk*.

Lanky and long-legged. "Western" Palm Warbler with rusty crown, yellow throat. Mostly beige underbelly with yellow undertail. Yellowish rump.

Eastern "Yellow" Palm Warbler more extensively rufous on crown. Bright yellow throughout underparts from throat to undertail. Yellowish rump.

Pine Warbler

Setophaga pinus

L 5.5″ | **WS** 8.75″

Present year-round in the Carolinas, the aptly named Pine Warbler runs the plumage gamut from the featureless gray juvenile to the burnished gold adult male. Almost always found in or around pine trees, Pine Warblers are large and heavy-set for warblers and move deliberately through pine boughs, alone or in mixed flocks in fall and winter. Most common in the Coastal Plain and Piedmont among stands of loblolly and longleaf pine, even in neighborhoods and parks with appropriate groves. Least common in the mountains, where extensive pine stands are fewer. One of the first birds to begin singing in spring, the cheerful, bubbly trill can be heard as early as mid-February, trailing off in summer when the birds are nesting and feeding young.

Stocky, with a heavy bill. Adult male surprisingly bright. Yellow throat, breast, belly. Dark eye with yellow eye arcs. Yellow-green head and back. Bright white wing bars on gray wings. Indistinct streaking on flanks.

Adult females grayer, but still with yellow throat, breast. Bold wing bars. Yellowish eye arcs. Some streaking on breast, flanks.

Extremely variable, sometimes with very limited yellow on throat, sides. Note eye arcs, bold wing bars, heavy bill.

Young females in fall with very little contrast. Wing bars thin. Bill long and heavy.

Yellow-rumped Warbler

Setophaga coronata

L 5.5″ | **WS** 9.25″

While a number of warbler species overwinter in the Carolinas, none are as numerous and conspicuous as the energetic Yellow-rumped Warbler. Hardy and ubiquitous, Yellow-rumps are found in a variety of wooded or brushy habitats from October through mid-May, typically traveling in loose flocks of a dozen or so and often joining resident chickadees, titmice, and wrens. They reach their greatest abundance in maritime forests along the coast, where they are perhaps the most numerous land bird feeding in the wax myrtles, whence the eastern subspecies, the "Myrtle Warbler," has its name. In recent years, the Yellow-rumped Warbler has been found breeding in the higher mountains of northwest North Carolina. Its call, a dry *chick,* is a common sound in fall and winter. Song is a series of twittery, slurred notes.

Brown and streaky, with bright yellow patch on rump Nonbreeding male with white eye arcs, clean pale chin. Yellow on breast sides.

Nonbreeding female with plainer face. White eye arcs, variable yellow on breast sides.

Breeding male present starting in April. Black mask bordered by white. Blue back with black streaks. White underparts streaked with black, yellow breast sides.

Yellow-throated Warbler

Setophaga dominica

L 5.5″ | **WS** 8″

A true bird of the south, the dapper Yellow-throated Warbler is a fairly common breeding bird throughout the Carolinas. Typically little more than a voice in the canopy, Yellow-throated Warblers prefer pine stands in the Coastal Plain and Piedmont, but are most common in sycamores in the mountains. They are almost always found near some body of water. Yellow-throated Warblers arrive early in the spring, singing on territory in early March, and occasionally overwinter along the coast from the lower coast of North Carolina south throughout South Carolina. The sweet, keening song is a series of descending notes, often rising at the end, *swee swee swee swee swo swo swup.* Call a harsh *shimp.*

Boldly patterned, with bright yellow throat and upper breast. Black mask and "sideburns." Large, long bill. White eyebrow. Plain gray back. Two bold white wing bars.

Black-throated Green Warbler

Setophaga virens

L 5″ | **WS** 7.75″

A golden-cheeked canopy-dweller, the Black-throated Green Warbler is for the most part a common breeding bird in the mountains above 2,000 feet in both states and a fairly common migrant elsewhere. The thin, buzzy song, *zee zee zee zoo zee*, often transcribed as *trees trees murmuring trees*, can alert a birder to the warbler's presence high in hardwoods. Easy to find along the Blue Ridge Parkway and in the higher mountains of northwest South Carolina.

Breeding male with bright yellow face and extensive black throat and breast, becoming coarse black streaks on flanks. Unstreaked green back. Narrow yellow band behind legs.

Females and nonbreeding birds with yellow face, pale throat, and black streaks on sides. Unmarked green back.

Prairie Warbler

Setophaga discolor

L 4.75″ | **WS** 7″

Despite the name, the Prairie Warbler breeds in brushy second-growth habitats, often with scattered cedars or young pines, in both Carolinas. Slight even by warbler standards, they frequently pump their tails. Present mostly from April through October, Prairie Warblers are most common in the Coastal Plain and Piedmont. Their distribution is scattered in the mountain counties, but they can be found at low elevations in appropriate habitat. Some overwinter, mostly in coastal South Carolina. Song is a thin, sputtering buzz, accelerating and rising into the higher registers, *zuh zuh zuh zuh zezezezezezeZEEEEE*; call is a heavy *chhht*.

Fairly small and slender. Male bright yellow with distinct face pattern, black crescent under eye. Black streaks on flanks.

Female similar to male, but more limited streaking. Less distinct face pattern.

Yellow-breasted Chat
Icteria virens

L 7.5″ | **WS** 9.75″

The outlandish Yellow-breasted Chat is technically a warbler, but few authorities really believe that it belongs in the family. Long-tailed, heavy-billed, and fairly secretive, the chat is a common breeding bird in overgrown fields with tangles and small trees, powerline cuts, and thickets at woody edges. The song, such as it is, is a series of disconnected squawks, whistled phrases, *chucks,* and *churrs*, unlike any other warbler's and more like mockingbird with a limited repertoire. In spring and early summer, the song is accompanied by a bizarre display flight with slow, floppy wingbeats and dangling legs. Present mostly from April through October, a few overwinter in maritime forests along the coast, where they can be quite reclusive. Call is a whiney *cheaw.*

Large, with a long tail. Bright yellow throat and breast. Bold white "spectacles." Stout black bill. Plain green back and wings. White belly.

Eastern Towhee
Pipilo erythrophthalmus

L 8.5″ | **WS** 10.5″

Boldly patterned and ground-loving, the Eastern Towhee is a common permanent resident throughout the Carolinas and a regular visitor to feeding stations. Prefers overgrown fields, woodland edges, hedges in residential areas, and other brushy places. Eastern Towhees can be found scratching through leaf litter anywhere in the two states, as much at home in maritime forests by the coast as on the highest mountains. Adult males in the north and west part of the region have red eyes, while those in the south and east are white-eyed. Call note is a hoarse, rising *jor-EEEE*, the song a familiar *PINK-o-EEEEEE*, often written as *Drink your tea.*

Long-tailed, with a thick, short bill. Male shiny black on head, breast, and back with chestnut flanks and white belly. Large white patches on tail corners. Birds in the Piedmont and west have red eyes.

Female similar to male, but with brown head, breast, and back.

Towhees along the southern coast and in the Sandhills regions have white eyes instead of red.

Bachman's Sparrow
Peucaea aestivalis

L 6" | **WS** 7.25"

A husky, long-tailed bird, the Bachman's Sparrow is, along with Red-cockaded Woodpecker, a classic species of the southeastern pine barrens and an uncommon permanent resident mostly in the Sandhills and the Coastal Plain north to southern North Carolina. Its habitat preferences are very specific, and it is found only in open longleaf pine forests regularly managed with fire to create dense thickets of wiregrass. Most easily found in spring and summer, when males perch atop shrubs singing their thin songs, a high-pitched single note followed by a melodious trill, *seeeeee chychychychychy*. Much harder to find in winter, when the species disappears into dense thickets. Sites like Sandhills Game Land and Green Swamp Preserve in North Carolina or Carolina Sandhills NWR and Santee Coastal Preserve usually have robust nesting populations.

Unstreaked breast. Richly patterned back with rufous, gray, and black streaks. Flat head with thick eyebrow stripe. Thick gray bill. Whitish belly.

Field Sparrow
Spizella pusilla

L 5.75″ | **WS** 8″

The cute, pink-billed Field Sparrow is appropriately named, a fairly common year-round resident of weedy fields across the Carolinas. Like most sparrows, it stays close to the ground, popping up on shrubs and saplings to sing a sweet bouncing-ball song, an accelerating *deew deew dew dew dew dedededede*. Most common in the winter, when numbers of resident birds are augmented by northern migrants, often among other migrant sparrows in thorny bushes and hedgerows. Call is a squeaky *ship*.

Clean gray breast, pink bill, and bold white eye ring. Rufous and gray on head. Streaks on back, with two narrow wing bars.

Chipping Sparrow

Spizella passerina

L 5.5″ | **WS** 8.5″

Ruddy-capped and clean-breasted, the small Chipping Sparrow is a common year-round resident in the Carolinas. It does well in all brushy habitats, from farmyards and open woods to parks and residential areas. Feeds mostly on the ground; it is alert and quick to flush into nearby trees at any disturbance. Nests close to the ground, often in dense young pine trees. Gathers in flocks of several dozen in the fall and winter, and can frequently be found in the rural parts of the Carolinas along roads running through fallow fields. Song is a mechanical trill, like the Pine Warbler's but less bubbly. Call is a simple, high-pitched *tsik*.

Breeding adults brightly marked. Bright rufous cap, black eye stripe, white throat, clean gray breast. Streaks on back. Gray nape. Black bill.

Nonbreeding birds brownish on breast and face. Crown dingier, streakier, with pale central stripe. Bill pinkish. Black eye stripe distinctive.

Young birds in summer and fall extensively streaked. Head pattern diffuse.

Savannah Sparrow

Passerculus sandvicensis

L 5.5″ | **WS** 8.75″

Short-tailed and heavily streaked, the Savannah Sparrow is a common winter resident of open areas from October through May, particularly in short grass-habitats with limited cover, such as fallow fields with stubble, overgrazed pastures, and sand dunes; this is the only sparrow commonly found so close to the beach. They flush easily, and put a great deal of distance between themselves and the observer, often perching up on distant fences or shrubs. Pale, sand-colored "Ipswich" Savannah Sparrows are uncommon on the Outer Banks. Song, heard towards the end of spring, a series of buzzes preceded by *tsip* notes. Call a flat *sip*.

Slender, short-tailed. Small yellow spot between eye and bill. Extensively streaked throughout. Fine dark streaks on white breast and flanks. Belly white. Back streaked tan and black. Bill pale.

Grasshopper Sparrow

Ammodramus savannarum

L 5″ | **WS** 7.75″

The small, short-tailed, bullnecked Grasshopper Sparrow is a bird of weedy fields and pastures with tall grass. Where such habitat exists, the species can be reliably found, but development and abandonment of farms have contributed to the loss of its habitat, and it is generally declining across the Carolinas. Perches on tall stalks to sing, an insect-like, high-pitched buzz preceded by tick notes. When flushed, short tail is obvious; appears like a ball with whirring buzzy wings, dropping quickly back into tall grasses and disappearing. Winters along the Coastal Plain, but easily overlooked when not singing.

Round, long-legged, and short-tailed. Flat head and relatively large bill. Unmarked buffy breast. White eye ring. Streaky back and crown with pale central stripe. Yellow spot at front of eyebrow and at fold of wing.

Nelson's Sparrow

Ammodramus nelsoni

L 5" | **WS** 7"

Both this species and Saltmarsh Sparrow were once
considered a single species, "Sharp-tailed Sparrow." Both
are winter residents of coastal salt and brackish marshes,
and are often found together. Common along the coast of South
Carolina into North Carolina to Cape Lookout, less common
northward. Almost any salt marsh hosts a few of these birds
from October through March, but they are fairly reliable
at Cedar Island NWR and Fort Fisher in NC, and at Santee
Coastal Reserve and Huntington Beach and in the marshes
around Charleston harbor in South Carolina. Unlike Saltmarsh
Sparrow, there are a small handful of inland records in the fall.
Calls of both are similar, a harsh, loud *chek*.

Short tail. Large, flat head with bold orange eyebrow
and moustache. Gray neck and crown. White streaks
on the back. Grayish bill. Buffy wash across breast
and flanks with indistinct streaks. Clean demarcation
between breast and belly.

Saltmarsh Sparrow

Ammodramus caudacatus

L 5″ | **WS** 7″

Like Nelson's Sparrow, the Saltmarsh Sparrow is a winter
resident of coastal salt and brackish marshes. But unlike
Nelson's, Saltmarsh Sparrow breeds along the Atlantic Coast
as near to the Carolinas as Virginia, and is more likely to be
found in warmer months as well. Common along the coast
of South Carolina into North Carolina to Cape Lookout, less
common northward. Fairly reliable at Cedar Island NWR and
Fort Fisher in NC, and at Santee Coastal Reserve and Huntington
Beach and in the marshes around Charleston harbor in South
Carolina, but likely in any similar habitat. Calls like Nelson's,
a harsh, loud *chek*.

Face similar to Nelson's but bill larger, yellowish.
Underparts whitish with distinct dark streaks
across breast onto flanks. Border between breast
and belly indistinct. Some birds with features of
both species may be unidentifiable.

Seaside Sparrow

Ammodromus maritimus

L 6″ | **WS** 7.5″

Large, dark, and possessing a beefy bill, the Seaside Sparrow is a fairly common year-round resident of coastal salt marshes. In the fall and winter, it can be found in just about any marsh along the coast of both Carolinas, but retreats to brackish marshes in the breeding season, likely to avoid tides swamping nests and chicks. Most common from the central North Carolina coast south throughout South Carolina, Seaside Sparrows can be found in just about any appropriate salt marsh, but are perhaps most reliable at Cedar Island NWR and Fort Fisher in NC, and at Santee Coastal Reserve and Huntington Beach State Park and around Charleston in South Carolina. Song is a strange, buzzy *turk-EE-ah-eeezzz*, call a low *tunk*.

Stocky, with short tail and very large, gray, bill. Dark gray overall with indistinct streaking. White throat. Yellow at front of eyebrow.

Fox Sparrow

Passerella iliaca

L 7″ | **WS** 10.5″

The chunky, richly-colored Fox Sparrow is a fairly common wintering bird, a favorite at feeders when poor weather comes to the Carolinas. Most of the time they prefer dense thickets and tangles adjacent to well-wooded areas. A later migrant than other sparrows, Fox Sparrows don't typically arrive until November and leave fairly early in spring. They are most common on the Coastal Plain and in the eastern Piedmont, scarcer farther west. Often sing on warm winter days, a series of rich, ringing slurred notes rising and falling seemingly at random, as if trying to find a pitch. Call, often given from the middle of an impenetrable thicket, is a hard *chhack*.

Large, with round body and head. Rufous and gray streaking on back, coarse rufous streaks on white breast and flanks. White belly.

Song Sparrow
Melospiza melodia

L 6.25″ | **WS** 8.25″

Easily the most abundant sparrow in the Carolinas, the streaky, long-tailed Song Sparrow can be found in a wide range of brushy habitats, from mountain balds to seaside forests to neighborhood feeding stations. A year-round resident in the mountains and Piedmont, it is mostly a wintering bird in the Coastal Plain but likely expanding as a breeder there, too. Like most sparrows, stays close to the ground, but males perch high in shrubs and hedges to sing, a few sharp notes followed by a musical trill, *plink plink plink T-WHEEEEEE tink*. Call is a burry *cheemp*. When flushed, flies in pulsing bursts, dragging its long tail behind it laboriously.

Fairly large head and long tail. Coarse reddish-brown streaks all over; dark on back and white underneath. Gray face with dark eye line, thick moustache. Streaks broad, as if drawn with a crayon.

Lincoln's Sparrow

Melospiza lincolnii

L 5.75" | **WS** 7.5"

Small and finely streaked, the Lincoln's Sparrow is often overlooked due to its similarity to the closely related Song Sparrow; Lincoln's are present in the Carolinas from October through May. Found in weedy fields and hedgerows; birders actively searching for sparrows can typically find one or two on the Coastal Plain. Most reliable around Lake Phelps in North Carolina, but not a sure thing anywhere. In October and November, they are most likely to be found in brushy habitats on the Coastal Plain and Piedmont. Doesn't sing in the Carolinas, but call is a rich *chilp*.

Similar to Song Sparrow, but slighter and shorter-tailed. Very fine streaking, as if drawn with a sharpened pencil. Buffier sides. Bill longer and more pointed; often shows a slightly peaked head.

Swamp Sparrow

Melospiza georgiana

L 5.75″ | **WS** 7.25″

The richly colored Swamp Sparrow is a handsome winter resident in wet fields, marshes, and bogs. Fairly common across the Carolinas from October through mid-May, the Swamp Sparrow is at it highest concentrations on the Coastal Plain, in both freshwater and saltwater marsh habitats. Often found in mixed flocks with other sparrow species, particularly the Song Sparrow. A distinct mid-Atlantic subspecies, the "Coastal Plain" Swamp Sparrow, breeds around the Chesapeake Bay and winters mostly around Mattamuskeet NWR in eastern NC. It averages slightly larger and darker than birds from elsewhere in the species' range. Call a sharp *pink,* like a metal coin against a tin can.

Fairly dark all over, with rich rufous-streaked back. Gray underparts, breast clean or with thin, indistinct streaks. Gray face and neck. Chestnut cap. White throat.

White-throated Sparrow

Zonotrichia albicollis

L 6.75" | **WS** 9"

An abundant and familiar winter resident and common visitor to feeding stations across the Carolinas, the chubby White-throated Sparrow is hard to miss from October through April. It prefers any sort of brushy habitat, from woodland edges to overgrown fields to well-vegetated neighborhoods, where it spends its time hopping around under sheltered shrubs, picking through leaf litter for seeds and insects, often in loose flocks of a dozen or more. Two color morphs are equally common, one with a bright white brow and the other with a more subdued tan pattern, independent of age or sex. Sings throughout the winter months, a plaintive descending series of whistles often transcribed as *Old Sam Peabody Peabody*. Call is a plain *tink*, like Northern Cardinal.

Large and fat. Brown-streaked back and wings. Bold head pattern with black and white or tan head stripes, small yellow spot in front of eye. Plain white throat, crisply set apart from clean gray underparts.

White-crowned Sparrow

Zonotrichia leucophrys

L 7.25″ | **WS** 9.5″

Plainly attired with a bold pattern on the head, the lanky White-crowned Sparrow is a fairly common winter resident in the western part of the Carolinas, uncommon or locally common elsewhere. White-crowned Sparrows prefer isolated hedgerows and brushy margins away from woods, typically in pastures and weedy fields and often near farms. Except in the west, very infrequent visitor to feeding stations in suburban landscapes. Sings throughout the winter, two or three clear notes followed by a short, buzzy trill. Call is a sharp *pink*.

Large and long-tailed. Distinctive head pattern with broad black and white stripes on the crown. Body unmarked gray, streaked brown on back and wings. Chin gray. Bill pink. Immature birds similar but browner, with tan stripes instead of white.

Dark-eyed Junco

Junco hyemalis

L 6.25" | **WS** 9.25"

This classic "snowbird" is a common breeding bird in the mountains of western North Carolina and extreme northwestern South Carolina. Elsewhere it is as a wintering bird, common in brushy fields, woodland edges, and well-vegetated neighborhoods. Often found in small flocks, frequently with Song and White-throated Sparrows, juncos hop around on the ground scratching for seeds and insects, constantly calling to each other with short little *tips, dits,* and *zits.* When flushed, they flash bright white outer tail feathers, distinctive among our common sparrows. Song, often heard along the Blue Ridge Parkway in spring and summer, a bubbly trill.

Large round head and short legs. Male is mostly dark gray, with white belly and pink bill. In flight, has bright white outer tail feathers.

Female similar to male, but washed out. Brownish gray body, darkest on head. White belly. Pink bill. Juveniles are common in the mountains in late summer. Extremely streaky with pale bill. Tail pattern, dark center with white outer feathers, like adult's.

Summer Tanager

Piranga rubra

L 7.75" | **WS** 12"

The only entirely red bird in the Carolinas, the gangly Summer Tanager is a common breeding bird across both states, particularly on the Coastal Plain. Prefers open woodlands, with no preference for pine or hardwood, singing a clear, jumbled series of warbling phrases from mid-story or canopy. Present from April through October, the vast majority of Summer Tanagers winter in the tropics, but a few have lingered into winter in recent mild years, primarily towards the coast, where they will come to suet at feeding stations. Easy to locate by call, a clicky *kittytuck* or *kittytuckytuck*.

Medium-sized and long-bodied. Head slightly peaked. Fairly long, heavy bill. Entirely rose red. Younger birds often with random green patches.

Female shaped like male. Typically yellowish-green overall, though sometimes grayer.

Scarlet Tanager

Piranga olivacea

L 7″ | **WS** 11.5″

Blood-red with velvety black wings, a male Scarlet Tanager is a breathtaking bird. A common migrant throughout the Carolinas, the Scarlet Tanager is also a local breeder in extensive hardwood forests in the western Piedmont and the mountains. Prefers to stay high in the canopy most of the year, feeding on insects in the treetops. Song is a series of burry, hoarse whistled phrases, like a Summer Tanager the morning after a bender. In winter, males replace their bright red with green, but keep the black wings. Fairly easy to find along the Blue Ridge Parkway and in the higher mountains of South Carolina from mid-April through October. Call is a hard *CHIP-burng*.

Male is striking and hard to mistake for anything else. Rich red with pitch-black wings and tail. Bill shorter, head rounder than Summer Tanager. Males in fall have green body, retain black wings.

Female olive-green with darker wings and tail. Head rounded and bill fairly short.

Northern Cardinal
Cardinalis cardinalis

L 9" | **WS** 12"

The cheery crest and sweet voice of the Northern Cardinal make it a perennial favorite. Very common across the Carolinas in a wide variety of habitats with some sort of brushy understory. Cardinals can be found in forest edges, overgrown fields, thickets, hedgerows, and suburban landscapes. Typically found singly or in mated pairs in the spring and summer, they form loose flocks of a dozen the rest of the year, often in the company of Song and White-throated Sparrows. Often take advantage of feeders in winter. Song is a series of clear, ringing slurred phrases of one or two notes: *cheer cheer cheer birDY birDY birDY* or *ritcher ritcher ritcher peer peer peer*. Call is a hard *tick*.

Long and lean, with prominent crest and long tail. Male bright red all over. Black mask encompassing eye. Orange-red bill.

Female tawny brown with red highlights on wings, tail, and crest. Black mask limited. Orange-red bill.

Young birds recently out of the nest similar to females, but lack mask, most red highlights. Bill black, turning red over the course of the first year.

Rose-breasted Grosbeak
Pheucticus ludovicianus

L 8″ | **WS** 12.5″

The boldly patterned, huge-billed Rose-breasted Grosbeak is a favorite at feeding stations in the spring. The species is a fairly common breeding bird in the western North Carolina mountains, and may breed in northwestern South Carolina. It prefers hardwood or mixed forests with regular gaps, and usually stays high in the treetops. Elsewhere, the Rose-breasted Grosbeak is primarily known as a migrant, moving north in mid-April and May and south in September and October. The song is a quick, musical warble, like a robin but faster. Most often detected by the call note, a high squeak that sounds just like a basketball shoe on a gym floor.

Chunky, with a short tail and very large, pale bill. Male (left) black and white with a red triangular patch on the breast. Female (right) with striking face pattern, large white eyebrow. Large, pale bill. Mostly whitish underparts with heavy streaking on breast and flanks.

Blue Grosbeak

Passerina caerulea

L 7″ | **WS** 11″

The deep navy blue of the Blue Grosbeak is a pleasant sight in old pastures, farmyards, and weedy fields with scattered shrubs and saplings. A fairly common breeding bird across the Carolinas in appropriate habitat, the Blue Grosbeak arrives in mid-April and sticks around through October. Often found around the similar, smaller, and smaller-billed Indigo Bunting, but note large bill and more purplish color in males. Song is a long mumbly warble at a low pitch. Call is a metallic *chink*.

Large head and longish tail. Male dark purplish-blue, can appear black in low light. Small black mask and very large, gray bill. Chestnut wing bars contrast with body. Some young males blotchy brown and blue.

Female tawny brown overall. Large head and very large bill. Reddish buff shoulder bar.

Indigo Bunting

Passerina cyanea

L 5.5″ | **WS** 8″

One of the most common breeding birds in brushy fields across the Carolinas, the turquoise-blue Indigo Bunting is a stunner. Present in the Carolinas from late April through early November, the Indigo Bunting nests mostly in overgrown fields and woodland edges, a habitat of which there is no shortage in the Southeast. Males sing throughout the day and throughout the summer, teed up on saplings or dense shrubs and pouring out a high, cheery song of repeated couplets, *wheer wheer teer teer tswee tswee*. Call is a lisping *thip*. Most migrate south, but a few linger through the winter, particularly along the coast.

Small and short-tailed. Male bright turquoise throughout, darker on head. Small gray bill.

Female dull sandy-brown all over. Mostly white on throat. Sometimes with faint streaks on breast. Bill small and gray.

Painted Bunting
Passerina ciris

L 5.5" | **WS** 8.75"

Impossibly ostentatious, the Painted Bunting is a mixed-up jigsaw puzzle of a bird. A fairly common year-round resident on the South Carolina Coastal Plain north to Cape Lookout, Painted Buntings prefer maritime thickets, and are usually found fairly close to the coast, though they come inland as far as Columbia in South Carolina. In winter they visit feeders as far north as the Outer Banks. Quite common at Savannah and Santee NWRs and Huntington Beach State Park in South Carolina, uncommon in North Carolina at Carolina Beach State Park and Bald Head Island. Song is a continuous warble, like Blue Grosbeak but higher-pitched. Call a short *pitch*.

Small and short-tailed. Adult male unmistakable. Bright red underparts and rump, blue hood, lime-green back. Small gray bill.

Female and young birds green, darker above than below.

Dickcissel
Spiza americana

L 6.25″ | **WS** 9.75″

A flashy, stocky bird of pastures and agricultural areas, the
Dickcissel is an erratic breeder in the Piedmont and Coastal
Plain of the Carolinas. Prefers weedy fields with little brush
and scattered trees or fence posts, where it sings its ratcheting
tick-tick SEE-o SEE-o song. Regular in the Carolinas but not
reliable at any one spot, Dickcissel will nest in a field one year
and be absent the next. Can usually be found around Lake
Phelps in North Carolina or in the fields around Townville in
South Carolina. In migration, can turn up just about anywhere
in brushy fields where sparrows congregate. Several records of
wintering birds along the coast, often among House Sparrows.
Flight call distinctive, a low buzzy *zernnt.*

Stout and short-tailed. Male
with bold face pattern, black
breast and white chin
surrounded by yellow. Yellow
eyebrow. Thick, gray bill.
Gray cheek and neck.
Streaked back. Chestnut on
shoulders. Female similar,
but without black on breast.

Bobolink
Dolichonyx oryzivorus

L 7″ | **WS** 11.5″

Strange in nearly all respects, the highly migratory and striking plumaged Bobolink is a fairly common migrant and local breeding bird in the Carolinas. In spring, Bobolinks sweep northward quickly in early May, stopping over in wet pastures and hayfields, particularly alfalfa, in flocks of many dozens. They can be found by watching for the piebald males to periodically shuttle around in large fields, many singing a ridiculous bubbling, wheezing warble that is hard to miss. In fall, the southward migration takes them toward the coast, where large flocks in sparrow-like non-breeding plumage pile into coastal marshes and fields. Nests in a few scattered wet meadows in northwestern North Carolina. Flocks are tight and fast-moving. Common call a rising *shwink*.

Male (left) is an "opposite bird," black on the underparts and white above. Black face with pale yellow nape. Black and white back with white rump. Female and fall-plumaged bird (below) sparrow-like but longer-bodied. Buffy face and neck. Heavily streaked on back and mostly plain underneath.

Red-winged Blackbird

Agelaius phoeniceus

L 9″ | **WS** 13″

The Red-winged Blackbird might be the most abundant bird in the Carolinas for much of the year. A common breeding bird in marshes, pond edges, and wet meadows, the rattling song, *konk-a-REEEEE*, is a common sound in any wetland habitat across the Carolinas. In winter most migrate to the Coastal Plain, where they form the core of megaflocks also containing Common Grackles, Brown-headed Cowbirds, and occasionally rarer visitors such as Yellow-headed Blackbirds. Such flocks contain tens of thousands of birds, occasionally hundreds of thousands. An irregular visitor to feeders in the winter. The streaky females are often mistaken for sparrows. Flies in loose flocks, calling a harsh *check*.

Lean with sharply pointed bill. Adult male entirely glossy black with a red shoulder bordered by yellow, mostly hidden when perched but readily apparent in flight.

Adult female dark and densely streaked. Superficially similar to sparrows, but larger, with longer legs and a shorter tail. Young males dark brown, with scalloped and streaked feathers. Limited red on wing.

Eastern Meadowlark

Sturnella magna

L 9.5″ | **WS** 14″

Oddly shaped, with a plump body, large bill, and short tail, the
Eastern Meadowlark is a widespread bird of open country across
the Carolinas. Prefers pastures, sod farms, and grassy fields,
generally without trees or brush. Most often on the ground, where
it strides through the grasses on long legs, but perches on fence
posts or power lines to sing. When flushed from the ground, tail is
clearly bordered by white outer feathers; wingbeats stutter. Song
is a lovely clear slurred whistle, *eeTEEo PEEdle-e-too*. Call a
buzzing *tzet*, like a toy hand-buzzer.

Pot-bellied, with long
legs, flat head, and short
tail. Breeding adult with
bright yellow underparts,
black band across breast.
Intricately streaked back,
bold pattern on head. In
flight, outer tail feathers
are white.

Rusty Blackbird

Euphagus carolinus

L 9″ | **WS** 14″

The inconspicuous Rusty Blackbird is a wintering bird of bottomland woods, forest seeps, and swampy backwaters. Locally common from November through April, the species has seen significant declines across its range in recent years for reasons that aren't clear. It still winters in fair numbers in the Carolinas, however, and flocks are found reliably on the Albermarle Peninsula in North Carolina and at Santee NWR or in the ACE Basin in South Carolina. Smaller numbers winter at wetland forest sites in the Piedmont and mountains, usually in flocks of a dozen or so. They are almost certainly overlooked due to their similarity to Common Grackle. Forages along the edge of water, picking through leaf litter and mud for insects or seeds. Call is an abrupt *chack*; song a series of squeaky gurgling notes.

Breeding male (left) in late spring becomes purplish, with little gloss. Round head and short tail distinguish it from Common Grackle. Nonbreeding bird (below) with variable blackish or brown body with brownish head, speckled throughout breast. Round head with fairly small, pointed bill and yellow eye. Female buffy all over.

Common Grackle

Quiscalus quiscula

L 12.5″ | **WS** 17″

One of the most abundant species in the Carolinas, the glossy, fierce-looking Common Grackle is hard to miss in any season in almost any habitat. A common sight in parks, neighborhoods, roadsides, or farms, Common Grackles strut imperiously across lawns or short grass, eating just about anything that can fit in their all-purpose bill. Often seen traveling in loose flocks in the summer, keel-tailed males in flight look like ducks flying backwards. In winter, many migrate to the Coastal Plain, where they gather in massive flocks with other blackbirds. Calls often in flight, a guttural *cherk*. Typical song a weird *hurk-hurEEK*, squeaky at the end.

Sturdy, with a flat head, long heavy bill, and long, keel-shaped tail. Glossy overall, but most colorful on head. Bright yellow eye. Females have slightly shorter tail, less iridescence.

Boat-tailed Grackle

Quiscalus major

L 16″ | **WS** 18–23″

Gregarious, outlandish Boat-tailed Grackles are common year-round residents along the coast of the Carolinas. Larger, with a much longer tail than the Common Grackle, Boat-tails are rarely out of sight of salt water, but can be found as far inland as Santee NWR in South Carolina. They take well to ornamental plantings in parking lots and neighborhoods, often scavenging for scraps at fast-food restaurants and around dumpsters. Male's display is impressively bizarre, with fanned tail, raised wings, and a long series of strange gurgling, popping, squeaking, and *zheet zheet zheet* calls. Calls are varied *chucks* and *clucks*.

Female brownish, with paler throat and breast. Yellow eyes and thick bill.

Very large, with an exceptional deeply keeled tail. Round headed with a large bill. Iridescence purplish or blue. Yellow eyes.

Brown-headed Cowbird
Molothrus ater
L 7.5″ | **WS** 12″

Much disparaged for its brood parasitism, the glossy, thick-billed Brown-headed Cowbird is nonetheless an attractive and common permanent resident throughout the Carolinas. Most often seen in farmland, neighborhoods, and open forests, the species can be found just about anywhere, particularly in spring when the female sneaks about looking for unwitting hosts for her many eggs. In winter, often joins large flocks of blackbirds on the Coastal Plain. Male's song is a strange liquid gurgle, call a short rattling chatter. In flight, travels in loose, mostly silent flocks.

Adult female (left) entirely gray-brown, paler on throat. Often with indistinct streaks on breast.

Chunky, with short tail and short, thick, bill. Adult male glossy all over, with rich brown hood.

Orchard Oriole

Icterus spurius

L 7.25" | **WS** 9.5"

Slender and quite small for a blackbird, the richly colored
Orchard Oriole is a cheery sight across the Carolinas. It is a
fairly early migrant both in fall and spring, arriving in early
April and departing by mid-September. In between, Orchard
Orioles prefer brushy second-growth habitats, woodland edges,
and fairly open areas with scattered short trees. Most numerous
on the Coastal Plain, less so to the west. Song is a rich jumble of
slurred warbling phrases. Call is a chatty *chirt chirt*.

Slight, with a thin bill. Adult
male with brick red breast,
belly, rump. Black head,
back, and tail.

Female mostly yellowish-green. Bold white wing bars.

Young males like females, but with black throat encompassing eye.

Baltimore Oriole

Icterus galbula

L 7-9" | **WS** 12"

The vivid Baltimore Oriole, famous for its flashy colors and long, hanging nest, breeds only sparingly in the Carolinas. Across most of both states it is a migrant, passing though in April and May and again from August through October. Nesting birds are local in the mountains, preferring open groves near rivers, with large hardwood trees. They are increasingly common on the Coastal Plain as a wintering bird, particularly at feeding stations offering oranges and jelly. Song is a series of well-differentiated whistled notes *tweedo tweedo plewdi tweedo*, parts of which are often given in winter as well. Call is a light chattering rattle.

Adult male with bright orange underparts and rump. Black head and back. Wings mostly black with white highlights. Tail orange with a black T-shape.

Adult female mostly dull orange, variably smudgy black on head and back.

Young birds in fall and winter variable, with orange and gray underparts. Usually brightest on breast. Gray back; wings with white bars.

Red Crossbill
Loxia curvirostra
L 6.25″ | **WS** 11″

With a large head and huge, cross-tipped bill, the dashing Red Crossbill cuts a distinctive profile. These impressive finches are uncommon breeding birds in the higher mountains of western North Carolina, and rare in far northwest South Carolina. They are highly nomadic, and can be difficult to cross paths with. Crossbills feed on spruce and fir cones, and can often be found in areas where trees are fruiting en masse. They are best located by their flight call, a bouncy *djip djip,* and once heard, one can occasionally find the big-headed, short-tailed birds flying by. Somewhat reliable around Mount Mitchell State Park and Grandfather Mountain in North Carolina, rare at Caesar's Head in South Carolina.

Compact, with a very large head and large bill with overlapping tips. Male (left) is rosy red, darker on wings and tail. Female (right) and young male mostly greenish, wings and tail darker.

House Finch

Haemorhous mexicanus

L 5.5″ | **WS** 10″

The drab little House Finch is appropriately named, as it is most common in parks and neighborhoods across the Carolinas, almost always near humans. Originally from western North America, House Finches first arrived in the Carolinas in the 1960s, where they quickly took hold. Now they can be found in all brushy, semi-open habitats, and they're regular year-round visitors to feeding stations. Song is a cheery warbler at a quick tempo, usually ending with buzzy notes. Call is a distinctive rising *schweeerp*. Distinctive bouncy finch flight, quick bursts of wingbeats interspersed with close-winged glides.

Smallish; short-tailed, with short, curved, blunt-looking bill. Male (left) with red forehead, cheek, and breast. Coarse brown streaks on flanks. Brown neck and back. Female (right) gray-brown. Plain face, curved upper bill. Coarse streaks on breast and flanks.

Purple Finch

Haemorhous purpureus

L 6″ | **WS** 10″

Sharp-billed and peak-headed, the raspberry colored Purple Finch is an annual but erratic winter visitor. In some winters, these northern nomads can be quite common, showing up at feeders across the Carolinas, while in other years they can be few and far between, or restricted to the mountains. Heftier and more finely patterned than similar House Finches, and with a larger, triangular bill, Purple Finches are particularly fond of tulip trees and sweetgum, and will sometimes stay close to areas where those trees are fruiting. Call a hollow *pip pip*, like a ball bearing in a soda can.

Female with white eyebrow and moustache. Streaking on breast coarse.

Similar to House Finch, but more distinct pattern on face, darker around ear. Slightly peaked head and straight, sharp bill. Color of male more pinkish, extensive on head, back, and flanks.

Pine Siskin

Spinus pinus

L 5" | **WS** 9"

Small, streaky, and noisy, the little Pine Siskin is another "winter finch" that can be unpredictable in its visits to the Carolinas, though it does nest in small numbers on North Carolina's highest mountains. Some years see siskins present in significant numbers, with flocks laying waste to bird feeders from mountains to coast. Other years they can be quite uncommon, with only a few reports. Prefers wooded habitats, particularly pine groves. Flocks are fast-moving and tightly packed, and flying birds have yellow flashes in the wings. Very noisy when present, call a rising buzzy *zzzzzzzzzZRRRRP*, like a fingernail running along the teeth of a comb.

Small; brown and heavily streaked all over. Yellow flashes in wings and tail. Thin, pointy bill.

American Goldfinch

Spinus tristis

L 5″ | **WS** 9″

Bright and lively, the little American Goldfinch is a beloved permanent resident of the mountains and Piedmont, and mostly a winter resident along the coast. Very common in open areas, particularly brushy fields, and frequently visits feeder in suburban areas. Goldfinches are voracious consumers of seeds, and are fond of fields with large flowers like thistle and purple coneflower. Song is fairly high-pitched and repetitive, with various chirps and *cheWEE* notes, often given as calls. Flight is bouncy, accompanied by a *per-too-too-too* call, often transcribed as *potato chip*.

Small. Breeding male bright yellow with black forehead, wings, tail. Bill pale orange.

Females and nonbreeding males similar. Yellowish-brown to gray body. Yellow wash on head and throat. Black wings with white wing bars.

House Sparrow

Passer domesticus

L 6.25″ | **WS** 9.5″

Abundant and conspicuous in urban areas and around farms, the House Sparrow is a native Eurasian species, introduced to North America over 150 years ago and now a permanent resident from coast to coast. Though it shares a name with our native sparrows, it is not closely related to them, being instead a member of a large, rather distantly related family found throughout the Old World. Along with the Rock Pigeon, it is one of the few species more common in cities than in rural environments, and bulky, big-headed House Sparrows are most often seen scavenging crumbs along city streets or at outdoor restaurants. Nests in cracks, crevices, streetlights, or any natural or artificial cavity. Call is a chirpy *chimp chimp.*

Short-legged; large, with round head. Short bill. Adult male with black throat and variable black breast. Gray crown. Rufous nape and back. Gray underparts.

Females mostly plain brown. Indistinct pattern on the head and darker eye stripe. Streaky back and plain underparts.

Author's Acknowledgments

My time birding in the Carolinas has been made immeasurably better by the people here with whom I've been privileged to have spent many hours in the field and in discussions about birds and birding. Their influence has shaped every page. The many names are too great to list in this space, but notable are Lucas Bobay, Susan Campbell, Jeff Click, Nate Dias, Ricky Davis, Kent Fiala, Nathan Gatto, Sarah Gatto, Sam Jolly, Mark Kosiewski, Harry LeGrand Jr, Henry Link, Dwayne Martin, Neal Moore, Pat Moore, Natalia Ocampo-Peñuela, Brian Patteson, Taylor Piephoff, Jeff Pippen, Kate Sutherland, Andrew Thornton, Mike Tove, and Scott Winton. For those who I have not included here, particularly the rotating cast of Birds & Beers participants, please know I appreciate all of it.

An additional debt of thanks is due to Ed Corey, Will Cook, Chris Hill, Paul Taillie, and Rick Wright, who took parts of my manuscript and made it clearer, cleaner, and more useful.

Thanks to Jeffrey Gordon, Ted Floyd, and my colleagues at the American Birding Association for the many opportunities being involved in the organization has granted me and their continuing work for birders in the Carolinas and beyond.

I greatly appreciate the guidance of George Scott at Scott & Nix, Inc.—it was truly a pleasure to work with you. Many thanks are also due to Brian E. Small, and the other extraordinary photographers whose images provide the backbone of this book.

Lastly, I am most grateful to my family, my wife Danielle and my favorite field companions, Noah and Julia, for their extraordinary patience, support, and good humor. And to my parents, particularly my dad, Greg Swick, who taught me to love living things, and to whom this book is dedicated.

—Nathan Swick
Greensboro, North Carolina
June 2016

Scott & Nix Acknowledgments

Many thanks to Nate Swick for his excellent text, and to Jeffrey A. Gordon, Louis Morrell, and everyone at the American Birding Association for their good work.

Special thanks to Curt Matthews and Joe Matthews at Independent Book Publishers (IPG) along with their colleagues, Cara Sample, Mark Voigt, Mark Noble, Clark Matthews, Jeff Palicki, Michael Riley, Mary Knowles, Cynthia Murphy, Aaron Howe, Lara Alexander, Jason Reasoner, Gabe Cohen, Josh Rowe, Mindi Rowland, Scott McWillimas, and many others.

Thanks to Alan Poole, Miyoko Chu, and especially Kevin J. McGowan at the Cornell Lab of Ornithology for their bird measurement data sets.

We give special thanks to Brian E. Small for his extraordinary photographs and to all the others whose images illuminate this guide, including Alan Murphy, Bob Steele, Jim Zipp, Joe Fuhrman, David Salem, Mike Danzenbaker, Reinhard Geisler, Jacob Spendelow, and the photographers represented by VIREO (Visual Resources for Ornithology).

We thank Rick Wright, Paul Pianin, Vicky Scott, Harry Kidd, and Sam Willner for their excellent work on the manuscript and galleys; James Montalbano of Terminal Design for his typefaces; Charles Nix for design; and René Porter and Nancy Wakeland of Porter Print Group for shepherding this book through print production.

Image Credits

[T] = Top, [B] = Bottom, [L] = Left, [R] = Right; pages with multiple images from one source are indicated by a single credit.

XIII–XXXIII Brian E. Small. **2–4** Brian E. Small. **5** Jim Zipp. **6** Brian E. Small. **7** Alan Murphy. **8–12** Brian E. Small. **13** Jim Zipp. **14–20** Brian E. Small. **21** Brian E. Small [T], David Salem [B]. **22–30** Brian E. Small. **31** Alan Murphy [T], Brian E. Small [B]. **32–43** Brian E. Small. **44** Brian Patteson/VIREO. **45** Geoff Malosh/VIREO [T], Alan Murphy [B]. **46** C. Nadeau/VIREO [T], Reinhard Geisler [B]. **47–48** Brian E. Small. **49** S. Young/VIREO. **50–67** Brian E. Small. **68** Brian E. Small [L], Joe Fuhrman [R]. **69** Brian E. Small. **70** Jim Zipp. **71–72** Brian E. Small. **73** Brian E. Small [L], Alan Murphy [R]. **74–79** Brian E. Small **80** Jim Zipp. **81** Alan Murphy [L], Brian E. Small [R]. **82** Jim Zipp. **83** Jim Zipp [T], Brian E. Small [B]. **84** Jim Zipp. **85–125** Brian E. Small. **126** Jim Zipp. **127** S. Elowitz/VIREO. **128** R. Curtis/VIREO. **129** Mike Danzenbaker. **130–134** Brian E. Small. **135** Brian E. Small [T], A. & J. Binns/VIREO [B]. **136,**Brian E. Small [T], R. & N. Bowers/VIREO [B]. **137** Brian E. Small. **138** Brian E. Small [T], Alan Murphy [B]. **139–150** Brian E. Small. **151** Alan Murphy. **152** Brian E. Small. **153** Alan Murphy. **154–156** Brian E. Small. **157** G. Bartley/VIREO. **158** Alan Murphy. **159–161** Brian E. Small. **162** Bob Steele. **163–171** Brian E. Small. **172** Alan Murphy [L], Brian E. Small [R]. **173** Brian E. Small [L], Jim Zipp [R]. **174** Brian E. Small [L], Jim Zipp [R]. **175–192** Brian E. Small. **193** Brian E. Small [L], Jim Zipp [R]. **194–195** Brian E. Small. **196** Brian E. Small [L], Mike Danzenbaker [R]. **197** Brian E. Small [L], Alan Murphy [R]. **198** Bob Steele. **199** Alan Murphy. **200** Brian E. Small [L], Mike Danzenbaker [R]. **201–244** Brian E. Small. **245** Brian E. Small,[T] Alan Murphy [B]. **246–258** Brian E. Small. **259** Brian E. Small [T], R. Curtis/VIREO [B]. **260** Brian E. Small. **261** Brian E. Small [T], Bob Steele [B]. **262–265** Brian E. Small. **266** Jim Zipp. **267–272** Brian E. Small. **273** Joe Fuhrman [T], Brian E. Small [B]. **274–301** Brian E. Small. **302** Brian E. Small [L], Bob Steele [R]. **304** Joe Fuhrman[L], Brian E. Small [R]. **305–311** Brian E. Small. **312** Brian E. Small [L], Jim Zipp [R]. **313–315** Brian E. Small.

Checklist of the Birds of North and South Carolina

The official checklists for both North and South Carolina are maintained by the Bird Records Committees of the respective states, under the umbrella of the Carolina Bird Club (www.carolinabirdclub.org). Birds noted with either (NC) or (SC) represent birds recorded only in those states. Those species without extra notification have been recorded in both states.

☐ Black-bellied Whistling-Duck
☐ Fulvous Whistling-Duck
☐ Greater White-fronted Goose
☐ Snow Goose
☐ Ross's Goose
☐ Brant
☐ Barnacle Goose (NC)
☐ Cackling Goose
☐ Canada Goose
☐ Mute Swan
☐ Trumpeter Swan (NC)
☐ Tundra Swan
☐ Wood Duck
☐ Gadwall
☐ Eurasian Wigeon
☐ American Wigeon
☐ Garganey (NC)
☐ American Black Duck
☐ Mallard
☐ Mottled Duck
☐ Blue-winged Teal
☐ Cinnamon Teal
☐ Northern Shoveler
☐ Northern Pintail
☐ Green-winged Teal
☐ Canvasback
☐ Redhead
☐ Ring-necked Duck

☐ Tufted Duck (NC)
☐ Greater Scaup
☐ Lesser Scaup
☐ King Eider
☐ Common Eider
☐ Harlequin Duck
☐ Surf Scoter
☐ White-winged Scoter
☐ Black Scoter
☐ Long-tailed Duck
☐ Bufflehead
☐ Common Goldeneye
☐ Hooded Merganser
☐ Common Merganser
☐ Red-breasted Merganser
☐ Masked Duck (NC)
☐ Ruddy Duck
☐ Northern Bobwhite
☐ Ring-necked Pheasant (NC)
☐ Ruffed Grouse
☐ Wild Turkey
☐ Red-throated Loon
☐ Pacific Loon
☐ Common Loon
☐ Pied-billed Grebe
☐ Horned Grebe
☐ Red-necked Grebe
☐ Eared Grebe

- ☐ Western Grebe
- ☐ Clark's Grebe (NC)
- ☐ Yellow-nosed Albatross (NC)
- ☐ Black-browed Albatross (NC)
- ☐ Northern Fulmar
- ☐ Trindade Petrel
- ☐ Bermuda Petrel (NC)
- ☐ Black-capped Petrel
- ☐ Fea's Petrel
- ☐ Zino's Petrel (NC)
- ☐ Bulwer's Petrel (NC)
- ☐ Cory's Shearwater
- ☐ Cape Verde Shearwater (NC)
- ☐ Great Shearwater
- ☐ Sooty Shearwater
- ☐ Manx Shearwater
- ☐ Audubon's Shearwater
- ☐ Wilson's Storm-Petrel
- ☐ White-faced Storm-Petrel (NC)
- ☐ European Storm-Petrel (NC)
- ☐ Black-bellied Storm-Petrel (NC)
- ☐ Swinhoe's Storm-Petrel (NC)
- ☐ Leach's Storm-Petrel
- ☐ Band-rumped Storm-Petrel
- ☐ White-tailed Tropicbird
- ☐ Red-billed Tropicbird
- ☐ Wood Stork
- ☐ Magnificent Frigatebird
- ☐ Masked Booby
- ☐ Brown Booby
- ☐ Red-footed Booby (SC)
- ☐ Northern Gannet
- ☐ Double-crested Cormorant
- ☐ Great Cormorant
- ☐ Anhinga
- ☐ American White Pelican
- ☐ Brown Pelican
- ☐ American Bittern
- ☐ Least Bittern
- ☐ Great Blue Heron
- ☐ Great Egret
- ☐ Snowy Egret
- ☐ Little Egret (NC)
- ☐ Little Blue Heron
- ☐ Tricolored Heron
- ☐ Reddish Egret
- ☐ Cattle Egret
- ☐ Green Heron
- ☐ Black-crowned Night-Heron
- ☐ Yellow-crowned Night-Heron
- ☐ White Ibis
- ☐ Glossy Ibis
- ☐ White-faced Ibis (NC)
- ☐ Roseate Spoonbill
- ☐ Black Vulture
- ☐ Turkey Vulture
- ☐ Osprey
- ☐ Swallow-tailed Kite
- ☐ White-tailed Kite
- ☐ Snail Kite
- ☐ Mississippi Kite
- ☐ Bald Eagle
- ☐ Northern Harrier
- ☐ Sharp-shinned Hawk
- ☐ Cooper's Hawk
- ☐ Northern Goshawk
- ☐ Red-shouldered Hawk
- ☐ Broad-winged Hawk
- ☐ Swainson's Hawk
- ☐ Red-tailed Hawk
- ☐ Rough-legged Hawk
- ☐ Golden Eagle
- ☐ Yellow Rail
- ☐ Black Rail
- ☐ Clapper Rail
- ☐ King Rail
- ☐ Virginia Rail
- ☐ Sora
- ☐ Purple Gallinule
- ☐ Common Gallinule

☐ American Coot
☐ Limpkin
☐ Sandhill Crane
☐ Whooping Crane
☐ Black-necked Stilt
☐ American Avocet
☐ American Oystercatcher
☐ Northern Lapwing
☐ Black-bellied Plover
☐ American Golden-Plover
☐ Snowy Plover
☐ Wilson's Plover
☐ Common Ringed Plover (NC)
☐ Semipalmated Plover
☐ Piping Plover
☐ Killdeer
☐ Mountain Plover
☐ Spotted Sandpiper
☐ Solitary Sandpiper
☐ Spotted Redshank (NC)
☐ Greater Yellowlegs
☐ Willet
☐ Lesser Yellowlegs
☐ Upland Sandpiper
☐ Whimbrel
☐ Long-billed Curlew
☐ Black-tailed Godwit (NC)
☐ Hudsonian Godwit
☐ Bar-tailed Godwit (NC)
☐ Marbled Godwit
☐ Ruddy Turnstone
☐ Red Knot
☐ Ruff
☐ Sharp-tailed Sandpiper
☐ Stilt Sandpiper
☐ Curlew Sandpiper
☐ Red-necked Stint (SC)
☐ Sanderling
☐ Dunlin
☐ Purple Sandpiper

☐ Baird's Sandpiper
☐ Little Stint (NC)
☐ Least Sandpiper
☐ White-rumped Sandpiper
☐ Buff-breasted Sandpiper
☐ Pectoral Sandpiper
☐ Semipalmated Sandpiper
☐ Western Sandpiper
☐ Short-billed Dowitcher
☐ Long-billed Dowitcher
☐ Wilson's Snipe
☐ American Woodcock
☐ Wilson's Phalarope
☐ Red-necked Phalarope
☐ Red Phalarope
☐ Great Skua (NC)
☐ South Polar Skua (NC)
☐ Skua species (SC)
☐ Pomarine Jaeger
☐ Parasitic Jaeger
☐ Long-tailed Jaeger
☐ Dovekie
☐ Common Murre
☐ Thick-billed Murre
☐ Razorbill
☐ Long-billed Murrelet
☐ Atlantic Puffin (NC)
☐ Black Guillemot
☐ Black-legged Kittiwake
☐ Sabine's Gull
☐ Bonaparte's Gull
☐ Black-headed Gull
☐ Little Gull
☐ Laughing Gull
☐ Franklin's Gull
☐ Mew Gull (NC)
☐ Ring-billed Gull
☐ California Gull
☐ Herring Gull
☐ Thayer's Gull

☐ Iceland Gull
☐ Lesser Black-backed Gull
☐ Black-tailed Gull
☐ Slaty-backed Gull
☐ Glaucous Gull
☐ Great Black-backed Gull
☐ Brown Noddy
☐ Sooty Tern
☐ Bridled Tern
☐ Least Tern
☐ Gull-billed Tern
☐ Caspian Tern
☐ Black Tern
☐ White-winged Tern
☐ Roseate Tern
☐ Common Tern
☐ Arctic Tern
☐ Forster's Tern
☐ Royal Tern
☐ Sandwich Tern
☐ Black Skimmer
☐ Rock Pigeon
☐ Band-tailed Pigeon
☐ Eurasian Collared-Dove
☐ Common Ground-Dove
☐ White-winged Dove
☐ Mourning Dove
☐ Yellow-billed Cuckoo
☐ Black-billed Cuckoo
☐ Smooth-billed Ani
☐ Groove-billed Ani
☐ Barn Owl
☐ Eastern Screech-Owl
☐ Great Horned Owl
☐ Snowy Owl
☐ Burrowing Owl
☐ Barred Owl
☐ Long-eared Owl
☐ Short-eared Owl
☐ Northern Saw-whet Owl

☐ Lesser Nighthawk (NC)
☐ Common Nighthawk
☐ Antillean Nighthawk (NC)
☐ Chuck-will's-widow
☐ Eastern Whip-poor-will
☐ Chimney Swift
☐ *Cypseloides* species (NC)
☐ Blue-throated Hummingbird (SC)
☐ Green Violetear
☐ Green-breasted Mango
☐ Ruby-throated Hummingbird
☐ Black-chinned Hummingbird
☐ Anna's Hummingbird
☐ Broad-tailed Hummingbird (NC)
☐ Rufous Hummingbird
☐ Allen's Hummingbird
☐ Calliope Hummingbird
☐ Broad-billed Hummingbird
☐ Buff-bellied Hummingbird
☐ Belted Kingfisher
☐ Red-headed Woodpecker
☐ Red-bellied Woodpecker
☐ Yellow-bellied Sapsucker
☐ Downy Woodpecker
☐ Hairy Woodpecker
☐ Red-cockaded Woodpecker
☐ Northern Flicker
☐ Pileated Woodpecker
☐ Monk Parakeet (NC)
☐ Crested Caracara
☐ American Kestrel
☐ Merlin
☐ Peregrine Falcon
☐ Gyrfalcon (NC)
☐ Olive-sided Flycatcher
☐ Eastern Wood-Pewee
☐ Yellow-bellied Flycatcher
☐ Acadian Flycatcher

☐ Alder Flycatcher
☐ Willow Flycatcher
☐ Least Flycatcher
☐ Gray Flycatcher (NC)
☐ Pacific-slope/Cordilleran
   Flycatcher (NC)
☐ Eastern Phoebe
☐ Say's Phoebe
☐ Vermilion Flycatcher
☐ Ash-throated Flycatcher
☐ Great Crested Flycatcher
☐ Tropical Kingbird (NC)
☐ Western Kingbird
☐ Eastern Kingbird
☐ Gray Kingbird
☐ Scissor-tailed Flycatcher
☐ Fork-tailed Flycatcher
☐ Loggerhead Shrike
☐ Northern Shrike (NC)
☐ White-eyed Vireo
☐ Bell's Vireo
☐ Yellow-throated Vireo
☐ Blue-headed Vireo
☐ Warbling Vireo
☐ Philadelphia Vireo
☐ Red-eyed Vireo
☐ Black-whiskered Vireo (NC)
☐ Blue Jay
☐ American Crow
☐ Fish Crow
☐ Common Raven
☐ Horned Lark
☐ Purple Martin
☐ Tree Swallow
☐ Northern Rough-winged
   Swallow
☐ Bank Swallow
☐ Cliff Swallow
☐ Cave Swallow

☐ Barn Swallow
☐ Carolina Chickadee
☐ Black-capped Chickadee (NC)
☐ Tufted Titmouse
☐ Red-breasted Nuthatch
☐ White-breasted Nuthatch
☐ Brown-headed Nuthatch
☐ Brown Creeper
☐ House Wren
☐ Winter Wren
☐ Sedge Wren
☐ Marsh Wren
☐ Carolina Wren
☐ Bewick's Wren
☐ Blue-gray Gnatcatcher
☐ Golden-crowned Kinglet
☐ Ruby-crowned Kinglet
☐ Northern Wheatear (NC)
☐ Eastern Bluebird
☐ Mountain Bluebird (NC)
☐ Townsend's Solitaire
☐ Veery
☐ Gray-cheeked Thrush
☐ Bicknell's Thrush
☐ Swainson's Thrush
☐ Hermit Thrush
☐ Wood Thrush
☐ American Robin
☐ Varied Thrush
☐ Gray Catbird
☐ Brown Thrasher
☐ Sage Thrasher (NC)
☐ Northern Mockingbird
☐ European Starling
☐ White Wagtail
☐ American Pipit
☐ Sprague's Pipit
☐ Cedar Waxwing
☐ Lapland Longspur

- ☐ Chestnut-collared Longspur (NC)
- ☐ Smith's Longspur
- ☐ Snow Bunting
- ☐ Ovenbird
- ☐ Worm-eating Warbler
- ☐ Louisiana Waterthrush
- ☐ Northern Waterthrush
- ☐ Golden-winged Warbler
- ☐ Blue-winged Warbler
- ☐ Black-and-white Warbler
- ☐ Prothonotary Warbler
- ☐ Swainson's Warbler
- ☐ Tennessee Warbler
- ☐ Orange-crowned Warbler
- ☐ Nashville Warbler
- ☐ Connecticut Warbler
- ☐ MacGillivray's Warbler
- ☐ Mourning Warbler
- ☐ Kentucky Warbler
- ☐ Common Yellowthroat
- ☐ Hooded Warbler
- ☐ American Redstart
- ☐ Kirtland's Warbler
- ☐ Cape May Warbler
- ☐ Cerulean Warbler
- ☐ Northern Parula
- ☐ Magnolia Warbler
- ☐ Bay-breasted Warbler
- ☐ Blackburnian Warbler
- ☐ Yellow Warbler
- ☐ Chestnut-sided Warbler
- ☐ Blackpoll Warbler
- ☐ Black-throated Blue Warbler
- ☐ Palm Warbler
- ☐ Pine Warbler
- ☐ Yellow-rumped Warbler
- ☐ Yellow-throated Warbler
- ☐ Prairie Warbler
- ☐ Black-throated Gray Warbler
- ☐ Townsend's Warbler (NC)
- ☐ Black-throated Green Warbler
- ☐ Canada Warbler
- ☐ Wilson's Warbler
- ☐ Yellow-breasted Chat
- ☐ Green-tailed Towhee
- ☐ Spotted Towhee
- ☐ Eastern Towhee
- ☐ Cassin's Sparrow (NC)
- ☐ Bachman's Sparrow
- ☐ American Tree Sparrow
- ☐ Chipping Sparrow
- ☐ Clay-colored Sparrow
- ☐ Field Sparrow
- ☐ Vesper Sparrow
- ☐ Lark Sparrow
- ☐ Lark Bunting
- ☐ Savannah Sparrow
- ☐ Grasshopper Sparrow
- ☐ Henslow's Sparrow
- ☐ Le Conte's Sparrow
- ☐ Nelson's Sparrow
- ☐ Saltmarsh Sparrow
- ☐ Seaside Sparrow
- ☐ Fox Sparrow
- ☐ Song Sparrow
- ☐ Lincoln's Sparrow
- ☐ Swamp Sparrow
- ☐ White-throated Sparrow
- ☐ Harris's Sparrow
- ☐ White-crowned Sparrow
- ☐ Golden-crowned Sparrow (SC)
- ☐ Dark-eyed Junco
- ☐ Summer Tanager
- ☐ Scarlet Tanager
- ☐ Western Tanager
- ☐ Northern Cardinal

- ☐ Rose-breasted Grosbeak
- ☐ Black-headed Grosbeak
- ☐ Blue Grosbeak
- ☐ Lazuli Bunting
- ☐ Indigo Bunting
- ☐ Painted Bunting
- ☐ Dickcissel
- ☐ Bobolink
- ☐ Red-winged Blackbird
- ☐ Eastern Meadowlark
- ☐ Western Meadowlark
- ☐ Yellow-headed Blackbird
- ☐ Rusty Blackbird
- ☐ Brewer's Blackbird
- ☐ Common Grackle
- ☐ Boat-tailed Grackle
- ☐ Shiny Cowbird
- ☐ Brown-headed Cowbird
- ☐ Orchard Oriole
- ☐ Hooded Oriole (NC)
- ☐ Bullock's Oriole
- ☐ Baltimore Oriole
- ☐ Scott's Oriole
- ☐ Brambling (NC)
- ☐ Pine Grosbeak
- ☐ House Finch
- ☐ Purple Finch
- ☐ Red Crossbill
- ☐ White-winged Crossbill
- ☐ Common Redpoll
- ☐ Pine Siskin
- ☐ Lesser Goldfinch (NC)
- ☐ American Goldfinch
- ☐ Evening Grosbeak
- ☐ House Sparrow

Species Index

Nate Swick is host of the American Birding Podcast, editor of the American Birding Association blog, and author of *Birding for the Curious*. An active Carolina birder, he has served as chair of the NC Bird Records Committee and manages eBird records for North Carolina. Outside of birding, he's an environmental educator and interpretive naturalist. He particularly enjoys patch birding in the western Piedmont near his home in Greensboro, North Carolina.

Brian E. Small is a full-time professional bird and nature photographer. For more than 25 years, he has traveled widely across North America to capture images of birds in their native habitats. He served as the photo editor at *Birding* magazine for 15 years. Small grew up in Los Angeles, graduated from U.C.L.A. in 1982 and still lives there today with his wife Ana, daughter Nicole, and son Tyler.

THE ABA STATE FIELD GUIDE SERIES

ARIZONA
ISBN 978-1-935622-60-4

CALIFORNIA
ISBN 978-1-935622-50-5

CAROLINAS
ISBN 978-1-935622-63-5

COLORADO
ISBN 978-1-935622-43-7

FLORIDA
ISBN 978-1-935622-48-2

HAWAI'I
ISBN 978-1-935622-71-0

ILLINOIS
ISBN 978-1-935622-62-8

MASSACHUSETTS
ISBN 978-1-935622-66-6

MICHIGAN
ISBN 978-1-935622-67-3

MINNESOTA
ISBN 978-1-935622-59-8

NEW JERSEY
ISBN 978-1-935622-42-0

NEW YORK
ISBN 978-1-935622-51-2

OHIO
ISBN 978-1-935622-70-3

OREGON
ISBN 978-1-935622-68-0

PENNSYLVANIA
ISBN 978-1-935622-52-9

TEXAS
ISBN 978-1-935622-53-6

WASHINGTON
ISBN 978-1-935622-72-7

WISCONSIN
ISBN 978-1-935622-69-7

Quick Index

See the Species Index for a complete listing of all the birds in the *American Birding Association Field Guide to Birds of the Carolinas*.